Simple Gratitudes

KJ Hannah Greenberg
with Rivka Gross

ISBN: 978-0-359-55803-2

Propertius Press
PO Box 3506, Martinsville, Virginia 24115
http://www.propertiuspress.com
email: admin@propertiuspress.com

SIMPLE GRATITUDES is also available as an ebook wherever books are sold.

Contents

Preface: Neither Riches nor Social Status

It's neither riches nor social status that makes our tenacious hanging on to life worthwhile. Rather, it's our integration of challenging "sensibilities," of deep feelings which might be sweet, but which are necessarily sharply disconcerting, that stretches us and that enables us to grasp the best qualities of this world. "Gratitude," not "entitlement," remains the proven route, within our mortal existence, to serving The Almighty and to finding joy in our service.

What's more, it both behooves us to see the entirety of our commonplace experiences as spiritual, and to elevate all off our spiritual happenstances. When we embrace our inspiration from G-d, our inspiration from others, our inspiration from ourselves, our inspiration from life's joys, and our inspiration from life's difficulties, we become fulfilled. Everything we encounter, no matter how seemingly taxing, is for our benefit. Our reaching great heights necessitates our grasping that our days and nights must be based on these sources of motivation to action.

Accordingly, *Simple Gratitudes* exists to broadcast the value of these sources as is articulated in the book's seventy instances of thanks. This assemblage means to raise our souls and to emphasize the importance of actualizing deeds of loving kindness. After all, no matter the nature of our lived deliberations, we are responsible not only to continuously push to do our best, but also to welcome all of the events that shape our personal evolutions.

So much work has yet to be completed in our process of releasing personal and social expectations and in replacing those anticipatory notions with simple faith. *Simple Gratitudes* invites us to live by working for The Boss.

Hannah Greenberg
Jerusalem, 2020

Inspiration from G-d

Divine Providence

The intervention of G-d in our lives is regular, but most often hidden. Sometimes, the masking comes from The Boss; sometimes, from us. Per the former, we can't, for instance, predict the nature of precipitation, self-determine our livelihood, or specify when we merit standing under the wedding canopy. Per the latter, we take for granted our ability to breathe, to walk, to laugh, and the like. In brief, there is an abundance of good in our lives, a plethora of instances of heavenly involvement, of The Holy One, Blessed be He, intervening. Unfortunately, there is a corresponding lack of our appreciation of such.

I recall, for example, a bus trip, which I took decades ago, between a regional airport and a major university. As the vehicle methodically transversed a portion of the United States' Midwest, I saw dark patches of maize plus lighter clumps of soy. Those fields ended only where they pushed up against industrial parks' strong fences. As a city girl from another zone, I had rarely sighted so many acres of commodities and had even less frequently witnessed agriculture and big business peacefully coexisting. However, the fact that those experiences were foreign to me did not preclude their veracity.

The big moments of life, like the smaller ones, are akin to those fields and to those outcroppings of businesses. Just because we can't even fathom the possibility of something occurring does not rule out its reality. I never thought I'd: have more than two children, become a religious Jew, or dwell in Israel. Bless The Name on all of those counts!

Not all of heaven's intercessions, at least not immediately, and at least not superficially, seem beneficial. When it's time to raise boundaries or to raze habits, most of us struggle. Although I would love to directly, and otherwise cost-effectively, reconstruct certain aspects of myself, like many folks, I falter. Embracing increasingly difficult exercises, in my physical therapy, after ripping my meniscus, giving up certain carbohydrates, after a receiving a dire set of blood sugar scores, and tweaking my bedtime, to reflect better sleep hygiene, all have been difficult changes for me.

In balance, intermittently, as I work to reach these goals, The Boss throws encouragements my way. While my physical therapy hurts, my ambulation is improving. I miss bread and potatoes, but I appreciate my increased rate of wound healing. I still feel like a kid and as such feel as though I'm missing something when I go to sleep "on time," but I feel spunkier on the mornings when I've had enough rest than on other days. I necessarily have to "walk the walk" even if I can't expect The Great Authority to grant my wishes; The Almighty, after all, is no bellhop.

Rather, it's up to our internal PR Departments to spin our understandings until we grasp that our challenges are growth opportunities. Personally, even when I make big efforts, I usually get imperfect results. My solution, ideally, would be to praise more and to complain less. Cognitively, I get the picture that our Father in Heaven wants the best for me and that G-d will always be there, spotting me while I struggle with my issues.

Concurrently, nonetheless, I feel stymied, stumped, and elsewise exasperated on a regular basis. I have to repeat over and again to myself that my perceptions can be illusions, that my efforts count, and that The Name wants me to be okay. Heavenly intervention requires a recipient. It's tough to place miracles if there are no vessels in which to store them.

The above notwithstanding, despite the fact that I know I am supposed to carry my personally assigned burdens, most often I'm unhappy during the early stages of tests. I rationalize, I minimize, and I deny my experiences i.e., I hang out with the evil eye.

I need people to be nice to each other at all times, so I act as though no one would take advantage of me. I want to slide into the glory of living in the Holy Land, instead of daily having to earn my place here, so I make little of living costs, of language barriers, and of creepy crawlies. I don't want my kids to be confounded in social situations, so I pretend the worse isn't occurring. These strategies don't work.

No matter the circumstances, I need to guard my mouth from spewing disagreeable words. No matter my perception of events, I need to trust that The Boss does and will continue to take care of me. My participation in the miracles of my life is my leaving aside my personal trash and making space for good, often "invisible" gifts. I can't directly alter the tilt of those around me, even if my self-made modifications positively impact them. I can't will

The Name to do what I think I need or want. I ought not to try to act that way.

Consider that no culinary institute graduate will ever make sauce from green apples as well as did my Eastern European maternal grandmother. No grammarian will write speculative fiction as well as does an award-winning colleague of mine. No upper middle class matron will appreciate the struggles of my neighbor, who runs her family's corner store. Yet, chefs still train, authors still publish, and adults still pursue sales careers; involving one's self in one's life remains essential. We cannot know which of our thoughts, words, or deeds is significantly weighty. We can only know that we must tread the middle of the road, no matter the apparent accomplishments of any other person.

It is insufficient, albeit necessary, to love and to fear G-d. Similarly, it is insufficient, albeit necessary to engage in acts of loving kindness and in other means of serving the worldwide community. It is rudimentary, though, to push one's self to partner in marvels great and small by dint of ongoing work on one's character traits. It's impossible to fully figure out miracles. We can't see what's hidden. We can't see what we refuse to view. We can know, however, that our working as diligently as possible towards achieving a goal is more than essential to experiencing the large amount of goodness that The Highest One has in store for us.

Immigration Special

Note: This piece was written on the cusp of our family making aliyah.

I am a Jew. My husband, too, is a Jew, as are our four children; Missy Older, Older Dude, Missy Younger, and Younger Dude. As it is said in that important line from *Psalms*, "If I forget thee, Oh Jerusalem..."

My family has experienced many life and death situations in the last ten years (death of a parent, pregnancy losses, etc)... We have relatives who know material abundance. We, ourselves, have known educational abundance. Yet, Computer Cowboy and I have learned that both money and social status are nothing in the face of what is truly important.

After our children were already in elementary school, we became fully *Shomer Mitzvot*, Torah observant. Subsequently, we enrolled our kids in local yeshivot (the oldest, Bless G-d, was even on a Torah Bowl Team, the next oldest was even invited to study "extra" *mishnayot*, tractates of Jewish law, with his *menachel*, his principal, and the two little ones, likewise, have been making us proud), and tried to contribute to our community. We engage in the welcoming of guests, try to help with arranged marriages, aid our synagogue (Computer Cowboy is on the board), and participate in many, many other types of other deeds of loving kindness (we just do what comes to mind without really making a list; it's enough that The Name keeps track).

We bought a house that accommodates Sabbath guests (since we are often blessed to have three tables full of people for most Sabbath meals. Hosting guests, in turn, allows us to perform additional mitzvot like introducing people to each other, building community unity, etc.—our friends are from all of our community's synagogues as well as from the part of our population not yet associated with synagogues) and we bought trundle beds so that our out-of-towners could sleep over. In brief, we are trying to do as many mitzvot as we can, as fully as we can, while we are learning more about The Laws. We want to serve G-d with all of our hearts, souls, and resources.

Computer Cowboy's boss asked if we would be interested in relocating to Jerusalem. There is only one answer; "yes!" We are waiting for Computer Cowboy's interview. We were told it could be days or weeks and that he might be expected to start work in Israel as soon as they make an offer. We were told that we would get half of his American salary and that he would have to continue to travel to India, as well as would have to travel back and forth to the USA.

We asked how soon he could have an interview. We are waiting.

Life is not about fancy things, although we are obliged to take care of our bodies as well as of our souls. Life is not about being important, though as the sentence at the end of the Jewish form of "Grace" reminds us, people who give to others never find themselves or their children alone, even when powerful beasts are starving.

We pray that The Name wants us to move to Jerusalem. We will do, without making an oath, everything we can (although I heard that jumping into the Red Sea, up to one's neck, is a chilly experience during this time of the year).

We are educated. We are resourceful. More importantly, we will bring to Israel a love and a fear of The Almighty and a love and a need to continue to give to other Jews. Presently, we mail packages to friends and give charity. We could do much more if we lived in Israel.

It would be far better to plant our four little trees in the Holy Land than it is merely to send our money. It would be far better for us to live with other Israelis than it is merely to write about how wonderful such a life would be. I hope we immigrate.

Effort, not Outcome

Our responsibility is to work toward resolving the struggles of our lives. G-d's province is determining the outcomes of those struggles. Said differently, we need to carry out our work as diligently as possible towards achieving our goals independent of whether or not we get what we want through the combined efforts of our wishes and our due diligence. That is, we have to endeavor to do our best when tested by the circumstances of our days and nights even though it has never been and will never be our prerogative to govern whether or not we receive what we think we merit.

Nonetheless, even though we are, ultimately, without control over the outcomes of our exertions, such that even though our lives might seem unfair, the endless unfolding of the universe remains, often in ways beyond our comprehension, a just unfolding. Subsequently, we suffer dissonance between what we prize and what we comprehend as taking place. We feel this discord at both personal and social levels.

Consider, as examples of this tension, the following situations that impact persons privately. In one case, a child was very ill. Her mother, a formidable challah baker and organizer of visits and aid to the sick, cried out prayers so often and so intensely that she needed to replace her *Book of Psalms*. The child's father intensified his efforts as a volunteer in many of the local synagogue's unacknowledged service positions. The child, herself, organized one Magen David blood drive after another and increased the amount of time she allotted for providing unpaid child care for poor neighbors. Nonetheless, her parents found themselves shoveling dirt over her grave.

In another case, a young couple and their progeny, new immigrants, who had had no intention of living among Bedouins, let alone off of the grid in any way, shape, or form, found themselves in a sparsely populated, Samarian hilltop community among a Jewish demographic that was new to them. Eventually, more and more families joined them at that height. When one such family was brutally attacked by ethnic cousins, the immigrants bought a dog. Whereas those settlers had no idea what the world, into which their children were growing, would be like, they knew that they had to remain located in that place that had grown to represent more than home.

In a third case, a young adult sought employment as a statistician at a government agency, or as an ecometrician, at a research and development firm. Principled beliefs disallowed that individual to look for work as a data analyst at fiduciarily-endowed corporations. As a result, that person, at least during the first year of his absorption, bagged groceries at a local branch of a large food store.

Consider, too, examples of the difference between what we idealize and what our lives realize. First, there has been an effort afoot, in the Knesset, to change Jerusalem neighborhoods' names to Hebrew. Since the contemporary Israeli government pays inconsistent tribute to the fact that Israel is the Jewish state, "*Mamilla*," "*Talbiya*," and "Holyland," currently bear Arabic or English labels. They could become, if the movement morphs to law, respectively, "*Hagoshrim*," "*Komemiyut*" and "*Eretz HaTzvi*."

In another instance, a group of Jews raised money to help the forestation efforts of this holy domain. Those funders had no idea that the organization to which they sent their monies looked the other way when ethnic cousins destroyed, and admitted to the intention of their destroying, thousands of dunams of plantings.

In a third instance, Israeli youth celebrated their enlistment in the armed forces as a chance to embody, literally, the mitzvah of protecting our land. Too soon thereafter, however, they and their families cried bitterly when those same noble young men were assigned to remove Jews from Jewish homes.

On the one hand, we could find solace for the discrepancies between what we believe ought to be and what we live through, by redefining the eventualities of our lives. We could, for instance, posit that no prayer is wasted and that, accordingly, the deeds of loving kindness, and words of entreaty, which escorted the aforementioned girl to the next world likely diminished the amount of affliction she will experience thereafter as well as will provide her with a higher level of attainment in The World to Come. Similarly, we could argue that while the forestation organization has a confused agenda, it does help to green up The Land of Israel, even if, at times, only nominally.

To some extent, however, such heartfelt words are no more than befuddled attempts to stay inspired. More true and more lasting good would be our claiming that loss hurts, in general, and that unfulfilled expectations leave us raw, more specifically. The only wiggle room we really have in negotiating our human condition is our choice of whether or not we accept what befalls us. Although there are sometimes difficult tenets to embrace, faith and courage serve us well.

It *is* possible for us to ascend from seemingly unworkable personal and social travails. Likewise, we can elect to conceptualize the most arduous of our moments not as deficiencies, but as gains; we can regard those hopeless points not as trenches, but as upward reaching treads by which we can arrive at higher levels of consciousness than the ones in which we currently find ourselves.

Granted, it is neither easy nor attractive, most often, to take on such a stance. In spite of that certainty, excusing ourselves from culpability for self-development, insisting that we try to stay only in places where we anticipate receiving comfort, is illusionary at best, dangerous at worst. It seems that the greater the centripetal acceleration of an event, the greater the G-force (in both senses of that word) that is realized by its participants. Instead of continuing any ill-advised habit of falling back on hackneyed excuses for giving up, that is, for yielding to impediments, when crises occur, we need to hobble forward.

This way is not easy. Our route is often not clearly marked. Yet, it is our job is to walk the walk and to let The Boss fathom the outcome.

Love, not Fear

Tonight, we stand before The King. We beseech our Father in Heaven to forgive us, to inscribe and to seal us in the Book of Life. We plead. We ask. We cry.

The good news is that we are loved. The bad news is that too often we approach our Creator from fear, rather than from fact. Older Dude zeroed in on this idea at my family's Sabbath table. He explained that if a kid spills chocolate milk, he can approach his dad through fear, shaming himself and pointing out his erroneous choice. Likely, his father will forgive him. After all, in apologizing, the kid identifies the behavior, says "sorry," and offers to clean up the mess, i.e., he makes rudimentary amends.

On the other hand, the child could approach his parent through love. He could point out how sad spilled milk makes his father feel, could take care of the mess, and then could extend himself, i.e., could do something more than wiping away the evidence of his mistake, to reinforce his connection with his parent. That "extra" might be, demographics depending, snuggling with his dad, rubbing his dad's back, or helping his dad take out the trash. Likely, his father will forgive him. After all, in apologizing, the kid identifies the behavior, says "sorry," and offers to clean up the mess, i.e., he makes amends. Better, though, in this second version of the scenario, the boy reminds himself and his dad that his mistake is only a small part of the much larger fabric of their relationship.

Whereas it is not our place to demand of G-d that we ought to be forgiven (though we can ask for as much), it is our place, and only ours, to remind Him that we have and that we hope to continue to maintain a relationship based on more than on our making errors and on Him forgiving them. Love breeds love. If we approach The King out of affection, we will find it relatively easy to continue to do so.

Fortunately, even if we had approached The King out of fear, we can change that aspect of our relationship to Him. There are no parents, of which I am aware, on Earth, or in heaven, who don't want their kids to relate to them out of love rather than out of obligation. Honor is required, but devotion is so much nicer.

While true adoration must grow organically from our hearts, there are practical steps we can take to nurture this feeling. The Nation of Israel came to (better) love The Name because of, not despite the fact that we have invested so much of ourselves in our relationship to The Boss.

The mom who has become accustomed to receiving pictures made in school, with which she regularly adorns her refrigerator door, and the dad who has become accustomed to being greeted, when returning from learning or from work, by lots of messy hands and kisses, misses those signs of fondness when they are absent. So, too, does The Holy One, Blessed Be He, miss the mitzvot with which we connect to Him when we become inconsistent in our performance of them. Unlike the angels, we were given free will; our affections, like those of small children, can't be anything but authentic. Humans are not automatons, Bless G-d.

In balance, our heavenly father is not a bellhop to be summarily directed by dint of our performing loving kindnesses. It is the case that sweetness (a theme of the High Holidays) is easier to embrace than is bitterness. A bonus is that our genuine demonstrations of ardor are often handsomely rewarded.

As an analogy, regard the sticky-fingered child, a son who regularly greeted his father when his father came home from work, but who had trouble getting out of bed one Sabbath morning. The dad could have left for *Shacharit*, the morning service, without his boy, instructing his wife to bring the lad when she came to synagogue with their younger children. Instead, the dad elected to be late to synagogue in order to show his son that his son was valuable to him.

Had the child been surly in nature or had he regularly displayed less affection to his father, likely, the father would have waited as a good parent is wont to do, anyway. However, the child's sweet disposition made it that much easier for the father to show his son compassion.

I suggest we make it "that much easier" for The Name to issue a good edict for each of us. Let's try to embrace Him with love, rather than hesitantly approach Him with trepidation. Heaven holds a cornucopia of blessings for each of us. Let's do our working as diligently as possible towards achieving this goal. Let's help insure we receive them. Our Father loves us.

Loud and Soft

I inhale. I exhale. Good comes in. Extra goes out. The rhythm of waves, of winds, of life's breath itself, builds on this patterning, on this configuration of converse energies. As we approach Yom Kippur, the holiest, happiest day of our year, we necessarily participate in the recreation of ourselves from such opposites. Loud and soft. Loud and soft.

Loud. We implore The Holy One, Blessed be He, to forgive us. We tried or didn't try to make *teshuva*, amends. We were aware or we were unaware of our slipping away from good options toward less desirable ones. We cared or didn't care if we improved ourselves. Despite all of our slip-sliding away, we want to live. We want to carry on. We want to go on inhaling and exhaling. So, with all of our might, we beg for the chance to do so.

Soft. Often, with seemingly minor amounts of energy, we try to repair the damage we have done to each other. We call, send an email, or seek out a friend so that we can offer a face-to-face apology. Even when we expend fewer resources toward fixing than toward breaking, we try to squash our egos, to reform ourselves into egos small enough to acknowledge, in the least, that we might, maybe, possibly, have been wrong and that we want to make over ourselves, that we want to take responsibility for modifications, and that we plan to implement them, immediately, in our interpersonal communication, specifically, and in our relationships, more generally.

Loud. We cry. We beat our chests. We prostrate ourselves on the floor. We point to ourselves literally, and figuratively, as repentant. We know our relationship with our Maker, too, has been less than right.

Soft. We think about the merit that forgiving another human being might add to the world. We consider how we can sanctify The Name, how we can contribute to His plan by being okay with, and by losing our anger and resentment over, another person's lapses. We can't let it matter so much: that others failed to meet our expectation, that they failed to make amends for the hurts with which they showered us, or that they lacked awareness that their hurts impacted us, or that they lacked awareness of how much damage that impact caused. We need to release our feelings regarding everyone else's stuff.

Such a mental state is a high level to which to aspire, but we ought to try to reach it, anyway. Otherwise, if we persist on being adamant that our perspective, tact, method, what-have-you is the (only) right one, we will remain very much alone. It's easy to admit we want to be reassured that Our Heavenly Father will stay by us. It's more difficult to admit that we want to be reassured that our human companions will continue to dwell by us, too.

Loud. The shofar cries, wakening our higher selves by speaking to our lower ones. The ram caught in the thicket, to replace human sacrifice, the sound of breaking glass, to substitute for torn flesh, the cry of a human instrument to pierce heavenly barriers; all are pedestrian stepping stones to exceptional change. We can overcome our shortcomings.

Soft. We reflect. Somewhere, in each of our souls, we accept that something or another in which we engaged, about which we spoke, or concerning which we thought, was stinky. We are not the goodie-goodies we wish we were, but are works in progress. The only faultlessness is, was, and ever will be that of The Boss.

Loud. Our hearts beat. Our breath comes in snagged streams; we gag, not for want of oxygen, but for want of opportunity to transform ourselves before His books are sealed and our mazel, our fortune, for a full year, is determined. Please G-d, we whisper, not on our merits, which are limited, but out of Your loving kindness, please inscribe us for all manner of good things. From Your vast kindness, not from our petty virtues, please grant us a full cornucopia of blessings. We want life. We want health. We want prosperity. We want peace.

Soft. We want so much. We struggle to believe that given our inadequacies the Almighty will be benevolent. Our faith is tested. Our trust is stretched. We were not benevolent. We slandered. We stole. We were involved in many bad moments, only some of which we regretted when we were involved in them, and only some of which we recanted even during these Yomim Noraim these High Holy Days. In fact, Dear G-d, most of us struggle to feel remorse over our flaws since we're still comfortable with them.

Loud. The sun drops in the sky. Our chance to appeal to The Name's compassion diminishes. We know pain. We feel stress. We somaticize, through the bodies, which The Highest One loaned us, the many ills for which we mistakenly used our souls to bring into the world. In letting the poison of our souls effect our bodies, too, we erred. Our transgressions need to become ladders to our Father, not tools of self-flagellation.

Soft. We entreat more. Only our prayer books and the voices of those individuals leading our services lift us. There is no more time to give charity before the end of Yom Kippur. There is no more time to enact additional instances of loving kindness before the end of Yom Kippur. At once, we are used up and newly born. As we experience our faults, we reach out to The Infinite for our renewal.

Loud. The final shofar blast ends our marathon of repentance. We remain standing. Literally. Figuratively. There's no rush to break our fasts; *Ma'ariv*, the evening service, is a welcome interlude between being spiritual paupers and returning to commonplace concerns. A few more verses of supplication taste so much better than does juice or cake.

Soft. Another year is here. The stars sprinkle the sky with faraway light. We smile at friends as we leave synagogue, weaker from our appeals than from our dropping blood sugar.

After our meal, we begin to assemble our sukkahs. We act on the hope that we were once more forgiven, that we can once more devote our inner stores toward simple, earthly concerns like structure and ornament, family and friends, that our imperfect service is accepted as a perfect sacrifice.

Loud and soft. The days and the nights of the New Year are inhaled and exhaled. They ebb and flow. In the coming days and months, we will make good choices and we will make bad choices. We will live as humans, breathing in, and exhaling both of those ends.

Holiday Joy

We're in a holy space. We've been granted at least a temporary reprieve for our wrong doings. Yom Kippur is behind us. A time of thanksgiving, a time of communing with seven of our important forefathers, a times of family and friends, a time of harvest and of joy, a time of not just holidays, but also a time of half holidays, a time of snuggling with our Father, once more, is our celebration of Sukkot.

Gratitude remains the proper adornment for our souls during this awe-inspiring period, during this span when we wander, with cleansed souls, through abundant celebration. Rare are the occasions during which our capacity to absorb goodness and the cornucopia of available goodness both overflow.

Now is when we are commanded to be joyous. This stricture does not mean we are to submerge other natural, but less exuberant, emotions or that we are to deny other normal reactions to life's challenges. Rather, this directive means we are to emphasize the positive.

Accordingly, I was thinking, with appreciation, about some of my experiences of Judaism in Israel, about some of my experiences of Israelis in Israel, and about some of my experiences of my family in Israel. What follows, thus, are bits and pieces of what were my smile-inducing thoughts. Whether or not my jottings also cause your face to break into an arc, I wish you a very easy time in fulfilling this holiday's charge to be merry.

First, for me, there is the matter of being Jewish in Israel. Consider that performing *tashlich*, a ceremony customarily performed by a body of flowing water, in which the previous year's sins are symbolically "cast off," in our desert realm, is a special experience. Up until this year, the synagogue, to which my family belongs, did not point toward a water tower, or toward a bucket for this rite, but elected to pray in the direction of a fish tank. Yet, this year, surprisingly, there was no fish tank in the building from which our membership rents. So, Computer Cowboy and I, on our own, after Rosh Hashanah, prayed at a fountain in a Jerusalem square. Only in Israel!

At least, our neighborhood's happy-making moments promise to continue on, per local tradition. During the intermediate nights, our community sponsors dance fests, that is, miniature galas during which men of all different head coverings, commingled with men of no head coverings, sway, bend, sing, and cry with enthusiasm. Those dads and sons, those students and teachers, those citizens and strangers, are not figments of an outside observer's interpretation of Sukkot and are not cartoonish figures from children's books meant to represent holiday ideals, but are breathing, sweating, rejoicing friends and neighbors. We have mazel when we are able to live as Jews in our Homeland.

Second, we live, Bless G-d, among other Jews, who have been fortunate enough to have resided in Israel for generations. Acculturation is a process. My ears perk up when people mention used bookstores that stock "English." I remain challenged when navigating Israeli roads (given regional driving behaviors, I am reminded, over and again, that I am not driving in Mumbai, in New York City, in Oz, or even in Shangri La).

In balance, the roughness of traditional Israelis' "understanding" of road rules is more than compensated by the softness of traditional Israelis' interpersonal communication. A kiss on one cheek is generally followed by a kiss on the other cheek. Small children look expectantly and trustingly to me and to other adults, with whom they've never before made contact, for help crossing streets. Seemingly standoffish guards remain great protectors. An unfamiliar person even gave my family encouragement by warmly asking, a few years ago, concerning our immigration to Israel, "why did you wait so long?" The Jewish People populate our home in splendid comportment. We're fortunate to dwell among them.

Third, counted among Israel's residents is, Bless G-d, my family. This year, thank-you, G-d, after communal holidays get tucked away, our personal parties will continue. Specifically, we have been invited to multiple weddings and to their related festivities during the weeks following the holidays. We are happily busy and busily happy.

Even after our friends' wedding-related festivities come to an end, that is, even after my family transitions from music, from Torah speeches, from friends, and from feasting, to alarm clocks, to chore schedules, and to the confused collections of leftovers in our refrigerator, fortunately, we will do so in Eretz Yisrael. What's more, my sons, my daughters, my husband, and I will continue, "yom yom," day-to-day, to be able to work to separate life's good episodes from life's strength-evoking episodes.

Consider that no matter how tall or how mature our kids grow, they continue on as persons seemingly designated to avoid "unnecessary" tasks. They offer their parents wisdoms such as "homework, Mother Dear, is not meant to be worried over," and such as "urban archaeology is overrated, especially in the form of cleaning our bedrooms." Sure, our offspring help Computer Cowboy and Yours Truly with government forms (while "neglecting" to translate teachers' notes) and sure, they do remind us, their parents, that whenever we choose to provide hospitality for neighborhood dumpster cats that we ought to inquire if those small mammals prefer cappuccino or straight shots. Yet, they gift us with a surfeit of dirty shirts, of kugel-stained aprons, and of bed sheets. It's wonderful! As a family, we're living as Jews in the Holy Land, in a good eye. We love all that is elevated about our circumstances and all that is mundane.

Quietly Now

The joyous tumult of the season of Rosh Hashanah, Yom Kippur, Sukkot, and Shemini Atzeret/Simchat Torah (Shemini Atzeret and Simchat Torah share a date in Israel) has passed. Crisper, brighter autumnal air cools my home. My family's thoughts turn back to school, to work, and to other mundanities. Nonetheless, in a good eye, the partying continues.

Given The Name's help, tonight and tomorrow will mark the weddings of young women dear to my loved ones. One bride is a close friend of our oldest daughter. The other bride is the child of two people my entire family adores.

In general, weddings elevate us. Even when our prayers seem to be "mere" infinite looping chants, our heaven-sent words get amplified by the authenticity of our rejoicing. It is lovely to be able to welcome new couples into our midst. It is especially sweet when we are invested in their lives.

I've noticed that people cry at nuptials. Deep within ourselves, we intuitively understand that what's going on elevates all of The Nation of Israel. It is so good to be Jewish! What's more, it's good to be Jewish in the Land of the Jews! I eagerly await those two weddings.

Meanwhile and more specifically, those two new brides are so special to my family that on Sunday and Monday of next week, respectively, we will, with G-d's Help, be making *Sheva Brachot*, postwedding celebratory meals, for them. My family is blessed. It is wonderful to be able to account for our time and money in a manner in which we can say that our resources are being used for happy and important events. It's great, too, to be able to share so intimately in such high occasions.

Besides all of that extraordinary hoopla, that is, beyond the onetime elations, we still get to celebrate Sabbath. This day of rest, of rejoicing in our connection to The Holy One, Blessed Be He, of reifying our ties to Him and to His Torah does not fail to show up in our lives when we are preoccupied with fine moments (or when we are preoccupied with challenging ones). Ours remains the positive mazel, every week, no matter that week's punctuation, that we get Sabbath. I love Sabbath.

In balance, my family experiences much the same fabric of living as does all other families. We are, for instance, currently still traveling through interpersonal and financial growth opportunities. We have a dearth of employment. We have significant health issues. On balance, tests make the happy items in our lives that much more poignant.

Compare and contrast the child who has a surfeit of food with the one who is regularly hungry. Likely, both children would enjoy a desert buffet, but the latter child, the hungry one, would appreciate the nature of that temporary abundance that much more. My family's hardships allow us a greater clarity with which to appreciate our gifts.

After all, this world, at best, is constituted by transitory "wealth." We humans are fashioned from dust and we will return, at the end of our days, to it. In between, we are tasked to appreciate our lives. So, we pray thanks and we work to grasp that we have everything we need, no matter the tribulations we endure.

Sometimes, Bless The Name, we have much of what we want, too. After our daughter's friend and our friends' daughter get married, with the help of Heaven, our own eldest daughter will be "the bride of the moment." In less than one month, Computer Cowboy and I will be privileged to escort Missy Older to her wedding canopy.

Our four amot, in a good eye, overflow with goodness. We are crazy about our groom (it doesn't hurt that he has sterling character traits). His entirely other soul is getting integrated into our family. Our child is gaining a superlative husband. Wow!

At present, I've not yet incorporated these data into my psyche. There will be the rest of my life to exclaim over this beneficence. I plan to take my time, to gives thanks, daily, for such fortune.

For now, I take sips from my understandings of more Earthly things. Before the wedding canopy, there will be, please G-d, a Bridal Sabbath. After the wedding canopy, there will be, please G-d, a week of parties. After the *Sheva Brachot*, our extended family plans to linger in our Homeland, to expand our time of celebration for a little bit longer. I am overwhelmed, in an astonished sense, with all of these forthcoming goings-on, Bless G-d.

I know that the month of Heshvan has the tradition of being a hushed time, a span empty of festivities, a period of slowing down and of regrouping, a portion whose calm allows us to recharge in order to spring forward during the coming year. Yet, this cycle, in my family, this month after we have tucked away the High Holy Days, thank-you Father in Heaven, has become a month of gearing up for additional heights.

I am polishing my dancing shoes, keeping my blender busy making dips, and singing my way through my days and nights. I'm not sure whether or not I am proceeding quietly at all.

More than a White Gown

Shavuot, the anniversary of the union of G-d and The Nation of Israel, the anniversary of His giving The Nation of Israel the Torah, is almost here. Similarly, spring is a time with a bounty of human weddings. Therefore, I began thinking about the association between the two.

A Jewish wedding is more than a white gown, a broken glass, or a billowing wedding canopy. When a Jewish man and a Jewish woman stand together beneath a matrimonial canopy, they are not only pledging their troth, but they are also elevating themselves, and by dint of that exaltation, elevating all of The Nation of Israel.

Just as Shavuot is the culmination of our nation's reaching, step by step, toward greater heights of spiritual unification, so, too, is a Jewish wedding the culmination of a couple reaching, step by step, toward greater heights of interpersonal attachment. An individual is as incomplete without their preordained help-opposite, the person who complements them perfectly, as are we, the Jewish Nation, without The Almighty.

Jewish wedding tradition maintains that akin to Mt. Sinai sprouting flowers in anticipation of the Jewish people receiving the Torah, a Jewish bride adorns herself in anticipation of her accepting her groom. Whereas a marriage contract might promise, on behalf of the groom, that his bride will be provided with food, shelter, clothing, and emotional needs, concurrently, his Jewish bride's mindful countenance promises that he will receive from her an understanding of Torah. In Judaism, "wife" is viewed as synonymous with "home" and "home" is viewed as the foundation of Jewish spirituality.

Accordingly, when a Jewish wedding is guided by custom, a bride telegraphs to the world that she means to endear herself to her mate. Her husband, in turn, announces, by means of the same, that he intends to fill himself with Torah. Modest demeanor in a wife is considered attractive to men. Torah learning in a husband is considered desirable to women.

So, the next time that you are smiling when: witnessing a *badeken*, a veiling of a bride; hearing *kiddushin*, the blessings of a betrothal; clapping after a newly formed couple exits a *yechud* room, a chamber designated for lofty seclusion; delighting in the tastes and smells of a wedding's festive meal; or are otherwise experiencing one of the many time-honored aspects of a Jewish wedding, consider that you are experiencing more than just the legal union of a man and his wife. You are experiencing, as well, an adoration that brings us closer to G-d.

Once More Down the Aisle

My husband and I have had the merit to attend many Jewish weddings. Some of those festivities abided strictly by Jewish tradition; others did not. No matter the nature of the goings-on under any particular matrimonial canopy, all of those events were joyous ones. Jewish marriage, after all, marks more than the connecting of a man and a woman; each Jewish marriage brings the Jewish People one step closer to The World to Come.

Whereas crass jokes have been made about the conjugal obligations of Jewish husbands, as those obligations are specified in the *ketubah*, the Jewish wedding document, truth be told, the physical form of attachment practiced by married Jews raises not only the individuals involved, but also the collective from which those individuals spring. In Judaism, we lift animal behaviors, such as eating and sleeping, bookending the consumption of food with blessings, and marking our waking up and our going to sleep with prayers.

So, too, do we exalt the basic human urge for physical intimacy by infusing that inclination with holiness. Judaism celebrates all aspects of personhood, sexuality included. However, we Jews codify our cravings. Per our laws, the fulfillment of the natural yearning for corporeal familiarity is exclusive to a man with his wife. We posit that the realization of the greatest human closeness ought only to take place per Torah stringencies.

On the one hand, we tout the joy of joining together as being a regular, necessary, and delightful part of married life. Whereas it might not be practical, it is legally possible, for a brand new groom and his brand new bride to fully consummate their relationship immediately after the rest of their Jewish wedding ceremony, in that room of lofty seclusion to which they vanish. No one smirks when a new couple emerges from that chamber. It doesn't matter whether the groom initiates a lifetime of touch by placing a piece of jewelry on the arm of his beloved or if he engages her in other kinds of agreeable activities. What matters is that we understand that connubial bliss is an essential part of being married and that we understand the vitality of acting on that mitzvah with immediacy.

On the other hand, it is common for well-wishers to applaud the husband and his bride when they emerge from their first instance of complete privacy. Those bonds, which the new couple has begun to form, link more than that man and his wife; those bonds link the rest of us, via our habit of obedience, to G-d. That is, a newly married couples' physical coming together brings our entire population closer to The Boss.

Consequently, every time my husband and I are fortunate enough to be guests at the weddings of our friends' children or at the union of our own dearly beloved biological or "adopted" young people, it follows that we also are fortunate enough to witness another occurrence of the Jewish People's allegiance to The Almighty. Each time that we observe a bride and groom promenading down the aisle, participating in Jewish wedding traditions, and then going into a reserved room to begin a lifetime of affection and devotion, we also are observing our own youthful passage to and from the wedding canopy, our own ongoing middle-aged commitment to each other, and the Jewish Nation's never-ending cleaving to The Name.

The Other Five

The Almighty gave us two tablets of commandments, half of which refer to *mitzvot bein adam l'Makom,* our relationship to Him, and half of which refer to *mitzvot bein adam l'chaveiro,* our relationship to each other. Whereas we are often conscientious about improving ourselves in the first category, i.e., about believing in G-d, about eliminating literal and figurative idols from our lives, about keeping The Name out of our less-than-polite remarks, about observing Sabbath, and about honoring our parents, we often slip from the center when it comes to the second category, i.e., when it comes to murder (okay, maybe murder is not such a problem), to adultery, to theft, to lying, and to coveting.

Examples of troubles in our interpersonal goings-on include: general, unbalanced speech, lack of mindfulness in marriage, and insensitivity in our business dealings. Praying three times a day or connecting with The Boss by keeping our heads covered or our food kosher is necessary for our inner wellbeing, but is insufficient to ensure our continued spiritual growth. Namely, if we allow ourselves to become desensitized to the point that we cheat our friends or neighbors, if we put our worth in front of the worth of others, if we become so wrapped up in our work, in self-pity, or in other self-focused matters, that we forget we are but an element of a greater community, and that we forget that our social connections are essential not just to the collective of which we are a part, but to our personal welfare to boot, then we are not climbing morally, but are heading toward a deep kind of *yerida,* descent.

To insure that our energies take us up, instead of down, we need to increase our beneficent interactions with others. Whereas acts of integrity are crucial to these exchanges, so, too, are thoughts based in humility and in compassion. It is not enough, for instance, not to worship media stars. We need, as well, not to desire the media devices possessed by our associates on which celebrities parade.

Consider that a child, who is given a box of crackers to share among her classmates, might manifest uprightness in her handing each classmate a comparable amount, might manifest meekness in not boasting about being the current snack monitor, and might manifest social concern in trading her own portion for the more crumbly portion of the last child she serves. Yet, she likely fails to grasp the gist of why it is commendable, let alone self-beneficial to act in those ways.

The young one has more to learn, over the course of her lifetime, about being a person of integrity and honor than she can glean from her understanding of her physical expressions of equity. It is bad to halt the development of truth at the stage of lessons integrated in kindergarten. It is better to layer an adult awareness of decency on top of our doings.

As evolving beings, it is essential for us to make a practice of *wanting* to engage in simple/mechanical kindnesses such as habituated donations to charity, and such as regularly yielding our seats to the infirm or elderly on public transportation, and in complex/focused kindnesses such as helping make arranged marriages in our communities and such as building bridges at festivities among various ethnicities of Jews. Our yearning to become upgraded beings counts in ways our acting cannot.

Mull over the notion that the weaving together of our lives with the lives of others can be tedious and can even feel thankless, yet it remains vital that we strive to plait our experiences with the experiences of others. Reflect on the exhaustion, for example, that accompanies sitting one or more times a week with a friend who has to endure dialysis. Ponder, for instance, trying to explain to very young children why certain questions are not to be asked of guests. Take into account, as an illustration, the wear and tear involved in helping a large segment of one's community assemble their sukkahs. Likewise, regard how providing shelter for a comrade, whose home is plagued by sewage flood, aiding an acquaintance in locating lost pets, or remembering to be quiet in synagogue can seem easier said than done.

Certainly, using our pocket change or our spare time to help food banks trumps our using those same resources to shop for trinkets. Counting to ten, before articulating anger, surpasses spending long minutes coordinating fancy clothes. Taking delight in the burnt chicken offered to us by well-wishers when we, ourselves, are incapacitated, carries us toward cultural sagacity. At the same time, trying to reach those ends or even thinking about wanting to reach those ends moves us forward.

Adultery, theft, lying, and coveting, to some degree, are omissions of proper thought. The friend, who made sure that the wheelchair-bound fellow was included in the circle of dancers at a festivity, modeled behavior for us. If we wished we had been him, we are, already partially him. The family member who hugged the hygiene-challenged visitor taught us how to respect others. If we wanted to have made that move, we already are on the path of having made it. The colleague who left a job rather than perpetrate dishonesty became our secret hero. If we laud, even privately, his behavior, we are already taking rudimentary strides toward emulating it.

We cannot fill our days and nights with too many random acts of kindness or with too many premeditated deeds of loving kindness. It is impossible for us to be too elevated when it comes to doing good deeds for our fellows.

The commandments focused on *mitzvot bein adam l'chaveiro,* similar to the deeds of loving kindness focused on *mitzvot bein adam l'Makom,* require not that we be golems of goodness, but that we infuse our choices with purpose. In coupling good intention to good acts, we advance our souls.

Gefilte Fish and Outreach

The other day, Computer Cowboy took me out for dinner. We chose a humble, Eastern European restaurant, where the service is excellent, where the prices are fair, and where the offerings consist of the sort of comestibles my grandparents would have eaten had they not been poor farmers in Belarus and Romania.

I ordered *p'tacha*, calves foot jelly, for an appetizer. My life partner, in the least, was put off by my selection. Yet, that man eats, nearly every Sabbath, ocean creatures that are chopped up, mixed together, and then jellied, i.e., he sups readily and regularly on gefilte fish.

Whereas I dined, for the first time in probably ten years, on my dish of fashioned aspic, my man chows down, nearly every seven days, on minced, emulsified sea bird. Aficionados consider such treats as the ones he prefers akin to or superior to *quenelles* and *kamaboko*.

Think about it; we Ashkenazim, we Jews descended from families most recently located in Central and Eastern Europe, tout the deliciousness of chopped pieces of water critters, combined with unidentifiable snips of carbohydrates, spices, and fat. We take this edible from glass pots, serve it up on fancy plates, and then consider ourselves to have cornered taste and tradition.

My point is not so much the way in which the appetizer, which is dear to my spouse, or the way in which calves foot jelly, which is a rare indulgence for me, are prepared or served, or why either item is not universally appreciated, but that what's appealing to one person might be disgusting to another. It's dumb to judge people according to their preference, or lack thereof, for dead bits of fin or for gelatinous portions of ox.

We can extend this concept beyond the pantry. Specifically, what works in outreach for some individuals is problematic for others and vice versa.

Every character trait granted by The Name can be used to serve Him. Some people, comparable to Rav Shlomo Carlebach, serve with song. Some people make Judaism more succulent by bringing sports to the fore. Still other people use theatre or cooking to create transcendental languages, to create routes to increased understanding.

Given that there is no prophecy in our generation, no person can know which individual, at which moment, needs our experiences, or which individual, at which moment, might benefit from them. Similarly, it is impossible for any of us to know which of our talents is the one that any particular Jew needs to feel cozier with The Almighty.

Yearning, which stems from that unique little spark in each of our Jewish souls, from that place within us that can never entirely abandon its connection to G-d and to His people, helps us secure our millennium-long chain. Such longing can and ought to grow from many things. The experiences we offer or undergo might or might not include: attending Agudah conferences, guesting at Borough Park weddings, enjoying the company of friends who do not laugh, too much, when we change napkins between Sabbath fish and meat courses, enjoying the company of friends who DO laugh, a lot, when we refuse "to cut" our first wigs, being welcomed to "special programs" on how to make Kiddush, being invited to represent our day schools on Torah Bowl teams, getting accepted into well-regarded *hesder yeshivot*, programs that combine advanced Talmudic studies with military service, performing National Service in Jerusalem's Old City, and on and on.

It remains the case that transferring our heritage can also include: not questioning why a holiday guest wears facial piercings, making bilingual prayer books available for Sabbath visitors, talking late into the night, on weekdays, with friends whose questions deserve privacy, encouraging newbies to help pack *shalach manot,* Purim baskets, for community elderly, building towering menorahs from plastic children's toys, inviting all comers to sit in our sukkahs, our booths, having challah bakeoffs, and much, much more.

Furthermore, sharing our wealth is not about numbers. Service to G-d is not about being able to verify, before acting, that our efforts will glean "success." Rather, our contributions need to focus on us performing at slightly better than our best.

Just as the Maccabees served by heart and not by number, just as Rabbi Akiva passed his heritage through a mere handful of scholars, not through his initial following of 24,000 learned individuals, just as Naomi and Ruth were singular persons, not vast coteries of women, and just as *Moshiach*, the messiah, will serve through the greatness of smallness, The Nation of Israel honors the partnership we cemented at Har Sinai not by promising magnificent feats to The Holy One, Blessed be He, but by accepting His Torah. Our job remains to embrace the totality of our passageway and only thereafter to learn (or to teach) its details.

Jewish history has never been one of grand paths to predicted results. Whenever we've tried to control outcomes, we've sacrificed trust, i.e., we've sacrificed one of our most important means of linking to The Highest One. Letting The Boss worry about the results of our hard work is a good flavor for outreach as well as is a sign of a good heart. We need to be keen to perform the first and to possess the second.

People hunt for religious connections not because they desire more of what they already possess in their life, but because they want to fill in gaps that they deeply sense. No more does the successful business person seek, from other Jews, a lecture on how to play the stock market than the teen with the tie-dyed hair searches for antidotes to hangovers. Yet, the former probably would be highly interested in lectures about the laws of commerce. The latter, equally, would be a good candidate for a celebratory table, which features talks about the need to guard the well-being of one's body and soul. Whether or not either of those persons is partial to gefilte fish or calves foot jelly isn't important.

In the long run, some Jews approach Torah through beautiful art. Others hear their own internal silver trumpets resound when they witness a simple act of kindness. No matter the route that takes Jews home, and no matter the number of Jews making that particular journey, the modes of outreach, which they embrace, are not to be judged. Like my husband's and my respective liking for appetizers, no introduction to the bigger meal, per se, is wrong.

Progress

Some of my dishes are packed. Others are not. Some of my linens are washed. Others are not. Incidental items, like my light fixtures, have been dusted, but my windows have not yet been washed. Yes, I am spring cleaning as well as am getting rid of *chametz*, leaven. Yes, my routine is highly imperfect both in terms of my execution of it and in terms of the sanity of my desired ends.

Beyond tussling with my maladapted ambitions, I struggle with my lack of help; half of my family has been out of commission with a nasty respiratory virus. I've brewed pots of thyme tea and have insisted that my loved ones take that potion alongside of their taking measured quantities of horehound tincture and of boneset (except for the thyme tea, which is not contraindicated for anyone except pregnant gals, don't even attempt these remedies yourself; plant-derived health aids DO have the possibility of grave side effects. Consult an herbalist). Yet, since my kids are big and my husband is a full-grown adult, only sometimes do my cherished others heed my advice.

It follows that we've yelled at each other, that family members have joined me in crying on the sofa, that doors have been slammed, and that words, of which none of us are proud, have been spoken. In our home, not only is it Passover Cleaning Time, it is also midterms. As well, my husband and I suddenly, and partially unexpectedly, are experiencing serious work pressures.

So, we've regrouped, repeatedly. I've modified expectations and have tried to cast off goals that seem unreasonable or that seem sound, but that remain unattainable. I dropped a class from my teaching schedule, too. My husband stayed away from his office while he was sick so as to get better faster. Some of the kids have canceled social appointments. All of us are cutting back here and there. Somewhere in the center of this performance array, the one marked by the poles of "problems" and "perfection," is the balance point of "progress," which I am trying to reach.

My husband and I have sat down and discussed with each of our children, individually, how many hours per any particular day he or she can be expected, realistically, to contribute. The days when a paper is due, when a midterm is given, or when a book's galley has got to get to a publisher, are times when wisdom dictates that my seeking less from family members, rather than my seeking more, is practical and kind. Similarly, the weeks when a business trip abroad has to be made or when someone has a fever, too, are times when high flying demands cannot sensibly be supposed to be met.

If we move none of the bookcases away from the walls, plant no new flowers in our empty pots (gardening tasks can be taken up again after *Sefirah*), and simplify our holiday menu, hence simplify our holiday shopping list, my family can still have a wonderful Passover. What's more, given those modifications, it is likely that we will arrive at our celebration with renewed harmony. Notwithstanding the fact that the weeks between Purim and Passover, for decades, have been our time to catch up on neglected household maintenance and improvements, this year we can't proceed per family tradition.

I reflect that some of the debris, i.e., the *chametz*, in my soul comes from being unwilling to accept that life is what is given, not what is ordered. This year, my separating the leaven from the unleavened can include my separating my obstinacy from my acquiescence. As one of my kids so wisely stated, "I'm not trying to convince you; I just want your permission." That child's words were a good reminder that I'm less than my best as long as I want The Boss to fulfill my wishes, instead of trying to bend my will to His.

If my Dear Hearts fail to grasp that preparations for our Festival of Freedom ought to be completed in accordance with my lists, and if they offer up alternatives, many of which are equally as fit as, or are even better than, my own ideas, *and* if The Holy One, Blessed be He, tweaks my experiences such that unforeseen tribulations get mixed in with my family's dust and bread crumbs, then my life is precisely as it ought to be.

So, five minutes or five hours from now, when my not-so-wee ones complain about the shelves of unwashed vessels that need to be cleaned and put away, when my help opposite gently whispers that this year, maybe, we don't have to hose down half of our street's sidewalk and that instead of searching for the perfect *seforim*, religious texts, we can buy parve chocolate for *afikoman* prizes, for trading for that half of a piece of matzo which is broken in two during the early stages of the Passover Seder and set aside to be eaten as a dessert after the meal, and when one of my dearest friends suggests, or more accurately insists, that I am long overdue for a break, maybe I could mull over heeding them. Those loves urge me to embrace alternatives out of level headedness and love, not out of meanness or spite.

During the next two weeks, while I continue to face down both personal and domestic cleaning tasks, I can remember to intermittently exhale, to sing or to whistle while I work, and to pray gratitude for one of my greatest freedoms, the blessing of family. No one else but me determines how I interact with my most precious people. I need to think and to say more "thank-yous" and fewer "not good enoughs."

About Passover and Giving Thanks

I think that gratitude needs to be practiced more often and concerning more matters. Sure, we mouth words of thanks, beginning with *"Modah Ani,"* "I Give Thanks," continuing with *"Birchot HaShachar,"* "The Morning Blessings," and onward, throughout our daily prayers. Sure, when we sit still long enough to observe, rather than to police our children, we feel glad for their existence. Sure, when our spouses fall asleep before we do, we look at their peaceful selves and say "thanks."

Similarly, when we or someone dear to us rises from a sickbed, we sponsor meals of thanksgiving. Sure, when we return from traveling over oceans or along dangerous roads, we offer up *"Birkat HaGomel,"* "The Prayer of Thanksgiving." Sure, when we experience a financial rescue, a marriage proposal, a pregnancy, or some other objectively significant goodness, we acknowledge our Creator. Nonetheless, most of us take most events in our lives for granted.

We're supposed to say "Bless The Name" at least one hundred times per day. Whereas big things, like being able to walk and to breathe are palpable gifts, so, too, are small ones. The hummingbird that flies three stories up to poke its beak through the screen of an apartment window is no less a wonder than is the golden hue cast, during a Jerusalem sunset, upon this city's limestone facades. A friend's child who learns to use the potty, and a cousin's child's first date, too, are miracles.

When making *havdalah*, the Jewish religious ceremony that marks the symbolic end of Shabbat and Jewish holidays and ushers in a return to the mundane, are we mentally racing to get on with the coming week, or do we look, after we say the blessing on the flame, at the proof of life that is the growth of our nails? More awe than is found in pyrotechnic-driven luminosity can be reflected in that moment of potential gratefulness.

As per the week, when the toilet overflows because a family member clogged it, or when we sigh, or worse, upon sighting a tower of unwashed dishes in our sinks, do we say thanks for the existence of our families?

When our friends interrupt our work efforts with phone calls or with audible Internet pings, do we praise the fact of our relationships?

This Passover, I had an opportunity to act with a modicum of extra grace. Like the majority of moms, I was living the shopping/cleaning/preparing/not-sleeping-enough portion of the year. I also had a very painful tear in my knee, which forced me to be sidelined and to trust my family to achieve my *balabusta*, good homemaker, goals.

Guess what? The house got cleaned. The food and the other needed accoutrements got purchased. The kitchen got changed over. The ritual service and ceremonial dinners got hosted. And, as has been our family's unintentional *minhag,* custom, not all of the matzo got eaten. In other words, Passover came and went very "successfully," independent of my personal state.

Not being able to measure my worth, and, more importantly, not being able to measure the many gifts that The Holy One, Blessed be He, bestowed upon me, by dint of the exoticness of the chicken dishes I might have cooked, by the amount of dust I might have removed from our blinds, or by the intricacy of the references that I might have foisted upon my children for their Torah speeches, was, in the least, humbling, and, in the most, perspective-evoking. Because I was forced to still myself, I was caused to ENJOY the holiday and to feel many levels of appreciation I might have otherwise missed.

For instance, during the end of Passover, my family had our happiness enhanced by one of our newer sons-of-the-heart. That spiffy fellow, a musician by trade, blended harmonies into our tableside songs, and, more significantly, occupied our home-from-yeshiva older son in countless games of chess. Most delightfully, whenever he, my husband, and my boys left for synagogue, I heard laughter.

As well, a daughter-of-the-heart brought over her intended. That sweet young man, whose sisters, we discovered while enjoying frozen strawberries, walnuts, and wine, had attended *ulpana*, religious girls' high school, with our older daughter, was witty, well-mannered and altogether charming. I whispered to our "adopted" daughter that my family thrills at making *sheva brachot*, the festive meals, which follow a wedding at which the *birkot nissuin*, the seven blessings, are said.

Meanwhile, that daughter-of-the-heart's younger brother, too, joined us for meals. That fine young sir learns at the same *yeshiva* as does his older brother, whom we adore, and as do many of the boys, whom we've merited to host over recent years. From that special youth, we received: juicy Torah, connection to his other siblings, regards from "our" *yeshiva* boys, and warm words from his mom and dad. As his next birthday is on an "out" Sabbath, I hope my family can bring his sister, his brother, and his sister's friend together, here, for at least one meal's worth of celebration.

The end of the holiday and the beginning of the same were not my only moments of appreciation. During the intermediate days of the holiday, while I was icing and compressing my injury, and while my husband spent time on "adventures" with each of our children, I took pleasure in my family's reporting on their trips. With one daughter, my spouse climbed around the ruins at Caesarea and ran along the beach. With one son, he cashed in some long dormant bookstore coupons. With another daughter, he lingered at a kosher-for-Passover coffee shop and talked about marriage, specifically, and growing up, in general. With another son, he enjoyed a meal at a kosher-for-Passover eatery, and bonded over: selections of dead cow, thoughts on the relative worth of various IDF units to which our child might apply, and ideas for *a cappella* music for *Sefirah*, the period of forty-nine days between the holidays of Passover and Shavuot.

Additionally, during the intermediate days of Passover, on noting that their mom was doing no better than limping, my kids got crazy in the kitchen. There was the latke cooking marathon (which ended with my husband making the batter into a large, delicious kugel), the salad wars, and the recitation of ways to use potatoes... I think they topped one hundred.

To boot, once separated from their brothers and from our intermittent male guests, the girls and their girlfriends hosted an evening gathering during which everyone sang. In a different space, our boys looked at photo albums. Elsewhere, my husband napped.

The holiday's middle brought family friends back to us, too. Although I was too grouchy from pain to encourage grown-up visitors, it was nice to have phone chats with loved ones who were living: in Jerusalem, in other parts of Israel, and in the States.

These days, I'm still literally hopping among specialists trying to find some means to reduce the severity and duration of my injury and to return me to normal life. Even so, my kids did a great job of packing up our Passover dishes and of unpacking our regular ones, of tossing items from the fridge, which I would have kept, and of keeping items, which I would have tossed. My holiday was more than special this year; I counted my blessings.

By the Hands of Heaven

Its two-thirty a.m. right now, six and a half hours before I have to be at the Central Bus Station to board a bus for a National Service seminar. I wasn't planning on writing a blog when sleep is of the essence, but life rarely goes how I plan it. That's why I stopped; stopped planning, that is.

I was never one for huge plans. I never sat down and wrote about what I want to do in the future or where I see myself in ten years. I did have a rough idea of how life was going to unfold. I was going to finish elementary school and get rainbow braces and platform shoes. I was going to get my driver's license at sixteen, and then a car for my birthday. I was going to have two sons who shared a room and slept on a bunk bed. I would kiss them goodnight, first the son on the higher bunk, and then I would bend down and kiss the boy on the lower bunk.

Needless to say, aside from the braces, life hasn't gone according to plan. And I'm perfectly fine with that. The twists and turns of life have offered me the chance to learn that everything is for the good, even if it's hard to see, at first.

It's the twists and the turns that I live for now. Life, according to my plan, would be bland. There would be no surprises and no faith. The fact that I don't know what's going to happen allows me to appreciate that everything is by the Hands of Heaven, specifically, is in G-d's hands.

I realize that the only control I have over my life is prayer and acting properly. I learn to believe that everything is for the good. It's not always easy to see the good while experiencing a lack of sleep, but I'm sure it's there, waiting for me around the corner, complete with a down comforter and two hundred squishy pillows.

As it's said in Yiddish, "מענטש טראַכט, גאָט לאַכט," "Man plans, G-d laughs."

— Rivka

There is no question that life is by the Hands of Heaven. Simply, The Name creates wonders, which are beyond our ken to conceptualize, let alone to execute. Miracles, from rainbows to babies, from interdependent species to interpersonal kindness, especially interpersonal kindness given to us by someone who, themself, is suffering, all provide witness to The Almighty's Benevolence.

Whereas effort is required to espouse prose about the glory of nature, about the glory of human nature, and about the glory of inner nature, a different type of exertion is needed to praise G-d while going through challenging times. When someone dies, for instance, we say "*Baruch Dayan Emet*," "Blessed is the One True Judge." When we wind up in Holland, even though we had a ticket for France, we say "g*am zu la tova*," "this, too, is for the good." In cases of unpleasant surprises, we necessarily must cry out our faith in The Name, i.e., we necessarily must cry out our belief that we do not, cannot, and never will control our lives.

I recall, years ago, when I had an academic book published, lots of speaking engagements at academic conferences lined up, a National Endowment for the Humanities award on my resume, and other accumulated professional accolades, I was convinced that I would be a professor forever. Instead, my funding for my teaching position disappeared (only to reappear two years later, when I was no longer interested) concurrent with Computer Cowboy's industry experiencing a downturn. In short, we had to stay where we were, geographically, in order for him to keep his then rare research post. Meanwhile, I could not work without relocating. We had no idea that G-d was streamlining our lives in order to prepare us to receive great fortune.

In short time, I became pregnant with the first of our four children. Had I remained in a seventy-hour-per-week academic position, it is unlikely I would have been a fit mother. It is possible, as well, that I would not have been able to conceive.

We were blessed to have one child after another. I was getting used to being "Mom," and hoped we would have a large family. Again, The Name had other plans. Our third child was born in a medical crisis and was admitted to a different hospital days later, with a diagnosis of two different possibly fatal illnesses.

Afterwards, between our third and fourth children, I experienced medical difficulties. What's more, during my pregnancy with our fourth and youngest, I made sixteen emergency trips to the hospital, never sure if that pregnancy would prematurely self-terminate or if we would merit a live, healthy baby. Bless G-d, Younger Dude was born at term and was born healthy. Two miracles.

Thereafter, inexplicably, I lost one pregnancy after another, often with hemorrhages, one of which was so massive that it found seven medics attending to me and a bucket waiting for me in the ER. Yet, that seemingly rough passage, too, was a window. From death, my husband and I found a means to strengthen our faith. In the end, we became religious Jews.

Accordingly, we moved to a community that accommodated our new lifestyle. There, too, our paths did not progress according to our plans. There, too, we thrashed about, inelegantly, trying to figure out how to control the picture. Of course the picture was never ours to control.

After despair of assorted kinds, we were invited to embrace aliyah, the elevation that is the immigration to Israel. Our perceived "losses," once more, were The Infinite's means of preparing us for greater things. Bless The Name, we are now in Jerusalem. The story does not end here, however.

Once Israeli, I taught a bit, but never found the career success I enjoyed in the States. Israeli friends, delighted with my storytelling, urged me to try out writing. I never told them I had chosen to be an English professor as a means of "funding my writing habit." I just abided their directive and reached out to some publications. Amazingly, the world reached back.

Bless The Name, in a little more than a year's time, I mailed my writing to dozens of venues, worldwide, print and electronic, religious and secular, creative and scholarly, and they, in turn, added my name to their rosters of authors. Very recently, I've become a reviewer for a few of those publications, and a columnist for another. Also, if it's okay with The Boss, in the very near future, I'll be teaching creative writing, online, in my dual capacities as a professor and as a published author.

Those events, too, do not conclude this story. Recently, in our nuclear family, the ground we held as solid has begun to shake. Something very good may soon be born from these tectonic shifts.

Today, my family recognizes that The Name Gives us agonizing experiences out of Love. Our job is to try to embrace His edicts.

I do not always or immediately succeed in manifesting acceptance. I keep trying.

— Hannah

Inspiration from Others

Small Packages

I didn't arrive at today abruptly, but rather via micro units called "days." My children didn't become teens and twenties all of a sudden, but in the drips and dabs of a lost tooth here, of newly flood-length pants there, of a fresh ability to stack plastic shapes, once, and of a rehearsed knack for stacking curfew arguments, many times. Any parental wisdom that came into my life came in trickles. Such measurements suit my grasp of family dynamics; my loved ones' shared journey is composed of patterns of small packages.

Consider that not too long ago, during a "typical" day in our home, they'd dash, after morning prayers, to the table to claim the "best" portions of diced bananas, or rush to the pantry to pack picnics resembling the miniature fortunes of "all of the other kids." My sons and daughters were sufficiently wee to take delight, to be entertained, and to otherwise be distracted by bits and snips of things. Tiny taters, berries, kisses, notes from Mom, all were regarded as "the good stuff."

As well, most of the miracles I experienced at that time, revealed or otherwise, were not the fill of thunder or lightening but the minutia of sufficient precipitation to save a daisy, or the tiny helpings of rebalanced electric charges that returned shalom to my family. We were focused not on grand gardens, but on marigolds that had been thumb printed into windowsill pots. We did not care about international publications, but about crayoned notes taped to our hallway's wall. Plants represented The Name's wonders. Words meant slight matters could have considerable consequences.

By regarding roots, stems, leaves, and buds, we talked about process, about the inevitable cycle of life and death, and about generations. By regarding the order and manner of human expression, we studied negotiation and cooperation. My sons and daughters were adamant on planting carrot tops and sunflower seeds, and on rooting sweet potatoes and avocado pits. They insisted, too, that we use "all of the polite words," and that when I made requests of them, those invitations fall within their self-assessed levels of ability. No child in our family was too small to clip rosemary or too little to discover dandelion's healing powers. Likewise, none of my kids was too young to be resolute about receiving a full share of "pleases" and "thank-yous."

Other developments within our home derived from modest quantities, too. The nutrition my kids most sought, way back when, whether packaged in sippy cups or straight from the breast, was the simple fluid known as "Mom Juice." Milk expressed for, but unwanted by, the family's youngest, whoever he or she was during a given year, was readily consumed by all other toddling parties. The kids appreciated liquid gold for what it was. No soda fountain treat or gilded vessel competed successfully against such basic wholesomeness.

Our sensibilities, the ones that positioned entities as less important than their component parts, however, led to certain awkward parenting moments. Many times, for instance, I encountered "roving bath products." Necessarily, Mommy's favorite shampoo, that bottle of herbal delightful, which I thought I had successfully hidden behind the organic lice spray, and for which I had paid premium at our local health food store, repeatedly went missing. Similarly, my slippers, socks, and sunglasses were objects of covet among the short set. Both my girls and boys retained an affinity for "anything that is Mommy's."

When I weeded a patch, that singular portion of our garden was where my children wanted to play. When I folded towels, that lone spot on our sofa was where my children wanted to jump. When I talked on the phone, they danced around my legs and under my feet. Basic acts took on new legacies.

What's more, that earlier span found me not only mopping up feelings and spilled cottage cheese, but also pulsing in rhythm to lunar winds and lunar tides; I was blessed to birth more and more children. Subsequently, I helped my offspring resolve more and more sibling conflicts.

When any two of my itty bitty people engaged in "territorial disputes," I'd vibrate my way across whatever space separated the combatants and send them to their corners. Dangerous or destructive matters, which passed over my "magic" threshold, transformed me into an incorrigible jay sounding off about springtime territory. Any single, unfriendly speech from my knee-high soldiers could cause me to caw shrilly for hours.

It follows that my kids were so bothered by my manner of adjudicating their "minor" misunderstandings that they raised their voices to protest my ministrations. Eventually, fatigued by their rhetoric, I'd be firm that they find ways to embrace whichever other lovely's view had distressed them. It didn't matter to me whether my children were fighting over who fed the cats, who failed to flush the toilet, or whose turn it was to pick out the bedtime reading. We needed peace, even peace arrived at in diminutive steps, in my familial kingdom.

These days, those same children, the ones who were well trained in the art of thesis, antithesis, and synthesis, work together. They are obstinate that their siblings corroborate their findings when any of them is held for bail on account of mischief (otherwise, it might prove awkward for them to retain their attraction to meandering felines, wayward lizards, and stray socks).

Fortunately, when they were kids, physical "fixes" were minor matters, too. When my loved ones suffered from stings, I used mud. I applied honey to burns, and heating pads to chests stuffed by bronchitis. Upset tummies were treated with fennel, ear aches with warmed olive oil, and mosquito bites were dealt with using oatmeal baths.

Not until the kids got older did we face scorpion stings, broken noses, and low levels of folic acid. Not until they were older did they go on school hikes, participate in MMA, or elect to become self-guided, i.e., junk food subsidized, vegetarians.

No matter the quantity of unmade beds, unwashed pots, and unidentifiable goop trailing from our family's microwave, I learned to regard such happenstance as almost inconsequential. Harsh responses would have cost me the invaluable closeness moms enjoy with their growing families. Rigidity, that is, large swatches of certainty, would have left me with only our salon's dust bunnies to listen to my blather. Contrariwise, these days, I like that my adolescents and young adults continue to seek me out and to talk to me.

Motherhood is an experience of constant adaptation, of ongoing balance. It is best transversed in small portions. When the kids pushed, I pulled. When they pulled, I pushed. Our dances, derived from familiarity, from trust, and from love, varied, over the years, by centimeters. Fortunately, those combinations of tiny movements continue to bring our lives together.

Starfighters

No polarized lens sunglasses or sweetly briny toilet water can protect me from the instant sensation of nausea I feel upon regarding their baby blues. The radiation with which parents and other superheroes need to be concerned has been, is, and will be—likely forever—their children's broadcasts.

Adolescents, typically, grump about their progenitors' lack of investment in fashion, specifically, and about their progenitors' lack of investment in consumer goods, more generally. Accordingly, kids' pouts and their other nonverbal protests produce powerful sources of fission, sources that are volatile enough to keep an entire continent glowing past midnight.

When their atomic rhetoric creates insufficient change, though, they try other strategies. One such ploy is their use of pseudo logic. Consider the following conversation.

"Mom, did you know that M54 was in the process of disintegration from the SagDEG?"

"I thought you were watching M20 in the Sagittarius Arm. Are you getting fickle?"

"Gotcha, Captain."

"Baseball scores are posted, by the way. Check out M8; same star type."

"Take me into the city after I finish commandeering the known universe?"

"Now?"

"Later. I'm only up to the Persius Arm. You promised I could play 'til we got to Orion. However, if you really loved me, you'd let me explore the Halo Globular Clusters, too, and the Andromeda Galaxy. Sam got to adventure there. His Mom is sooo cool."

"Me too; I'm as cool as liquid nitrogen. If you so much as investigate the Canis Major Dwarf, you will get an extra day's worth of garbage duty. *Comprende*?"

"Space is a deep and dark thing, Mom."

At times, when my children try to push my buttons, I make use of parental defenses. My favorite contingency strategy is to write about my sons and daughters.

Once, for instance, when "school" had become a forbidden topic for reasons not possible for my generation to grasp, I helplessly watched two of my gang alternate between sitting on the sofa and crying and storming into their respective rooms. In response, I ran to my keyboard.

There is weird comfort, for me, in exposing the nuances of my kids' adolescent behaviors to strangers. Verbs at full mast, I chirped to my unknown audience about my confusion, regarding my lack of understanding concerning a child, who, in a good eye, reaped 90's on two major tests, but was brought to tears over another one, and regarding that child's sibling, who, in a good eye, was improving a door slamming reflex because that sibling had maximized the bonus points, which that one's teacher was willing to offer, i.e., would not be "paid" for academic achievement any longer..

As I filled pages with nouns and adjectives, I was able to find the sort of serenity that enables parents to shove yet one more unmatched sock into an already burgeoning drawer and to collect, without denouncing their scion, the pillows that inevitably land behind the sofas.

Nonetheless, my writing was suddenly interrupted. Having sounded off with tears and crashes, the kids were voicing their remonstrations by parading back and forth to the family fridge and to the family phone. Each time, though, that they passed my office, they announced their dissatisfaction.

Their pleasure trips became, to me, disagreeable excursions. I became grouchier and grouchier. Every ten or fifteen minutes, someone sought my nonverbal acknowledgment. Every ten or fifteen minutes, someone knocked on my office door.

I countered. I shot back with distraction. They were to wash the windows, the mirrors, and the cat. Given that we had no cat, I thought their energies might be redirected for at least half of an hour.

In response, they slid papers under my door. Their pages were filled with tales about turkey hens with a taste for tapioca chips mixed with oil cakes, and with tales of an invisible Komodo dragon that pointedly pursued my prickle of imaginary hedgehogs. As well, my kids shoved over my lintel illustrations of gum tragacanth ribboning out of plants and illustrations of a first class starship exploding in space.

I began to consider the merits of my own supernovaing. New familial constellations could become visible once the obscuring dust clouds shifted. Maybe intergalactic vessels would not be the only items detonating that day.

Just before my cataclysmic meltdown, I was able to calm down. Maybe, my children needed hugs. Maybe, they needed *discipline*. Maybe, they needed tomato rice soup. Maybe, my kids were trying their best to communicate to me.

I dialed the house phone from my office and insisted that my voice be switched to the loudspeaker. "This is your commander. Over."

"What Mom?"

"I will cease writing about you, for the benefit of people we will never meet, long enough to cook soup and chop salad. Over."

"Will you brown the onions first?"

"Maybe. Over."

"Will you drive me to the mall?"

"Not today. Over."

"Can you cut out half of our chores?"

"Are you crazy? Over."

"Can we fly with you?"

"My pleasure. Over."

Growing Up

This past Sabbath, I was blessed to have all of my sons and daughters home. I recognized this confluence of circumstances for the increasing rarity that it is. The eldest is in "the marriage portion," and will, accordingly, I pray, soon find the person who will complement her perfectly and then she will move on to her own home. The next eldest spends most of his Sabbaths at his *hesder yeshiva*. What's more, next year, he'll enter the army. The third has just one year and a bit left of high school before she enters National Service. My baby is no baby any longer, but a young man of fourteen, in a good eye.

Plus, this past Sabbath, Computer Cowboy was, unfortunately, abroad. Although he was able to spend Sabbath with our former community, he was not able to share in our family time. Usually, my help-opposite is able to tweak his travel schedule to get home to greet the Sabbath Queen with us. Not so, this past week.

As a result of all of the above, combined with my choice not to invite guests to our home, last Sabbath, I was returned to a former gratification about my children; I was returned to feeling happy and proud about them. After releasing myself from academia, I had spent more than a dozen years focused on raising them, but then they grew up and I concentrated on creative writing. It has been a long time since I simultaneously, yet exclusively, paid each of them attention.

Thus, I found myself, last Friday afternoon, sitting at our table and crying. I smiled through the tears and told my sons and daughters I was feeling joyous. They tried to tell me jokes, to introduce entertainments, of which they knew I disapproved, and to otherwise distract me from my strong feelings. I laughed at their funny remarks and then cried even more robustly. Even when I asked them to shut their electronics, I continued to drip tears.

They might be, respectively, looking with the good eye, 21, 19, 16, and 14, but suddenly I could see through their attained physical height, through their academic accomplishments, through their skills with friends, and through their many and varied tribulations, some conquered, others some still "in process," to their *souls*. They were at once 10 going on 21, 8 going on 19, 5 going on 16, and 3 going on 14.

They were, concurrently, in braces, but in the latest fashion, nervous about reciting a simple blessing in Hebrew, but glorying in giving over complicated Torah speeches, trying to act "like big kids," but confident in their exchanges with their siblings, and able to politely disagree with their primary care provider, but still a tad unsure of how to hold onto their own opinions. Before my eyes, their geographic, worldview, and other differences melted and they became, all at once, the boys and girls who had dug holes in the family backyard, who had fought over whose turn it was to sit by the car's windows, and who had delighted in pulling their cookies apart.

Instantly, I was transported to a world where our greatest stresses had included: making sure everyone took afternoon naps, certifying that the allergic among us had enough rice cakes to substitute for bread and enough calcium-enriched rice juice to substitute for milk, and checking that relatives always received thank-you notes or calls for gifts that the kids received. Whereas, at that time, the diapers, the potty minutes, and the need to search for clean public bathrooms seemed unrelenting, and whereas the amount of hours I spent lining up stuffed animals "just so" seemed to extend into infinity, in truth, I didn't get enough muddy shoes, handprints on windows, spilled sippy cups, or forts built from sofa pillows.

I might have complained, at the time, about the seemingly endless laundry or about having to read certain picture books again and again and again and again, but in actual fact, I never felt that setting aside a hard-won professional career for mommyhood or that spending nearly a decade and a half in sleep deprivation mode were much of a cost for all of the contentment, pleasure, and soothing of spirit that I gathered from my children. In reality, I considered and continue to consider myself among the most fortunate of humans as I was granted those delights in this world, rather than having to wait for the possibility of them in the world to come.

So, last week, before Sabbath, I bawled. I smiled. I cried some more. There is much joy to be had in this lifetime. Some aspects of it come from our relationship to The Name. Other aspects of it come from our relationship to each other. Certainly a mother's association with her children and their association with each other have been, are, and will continue to be primal sources of good feeling.

Relative Riches: Familial Transitions

It's not possible to fully appreciate what we have before it's taken away. Certainly, we might have gratitude for the goodness in our lives. Of course, we might give thanks for our abundance. Yet, it is not within human ken to be entirely able, in this world, to realize the value of our blessings.

A few months ago, my husband and our older son got into our car and drove away. They traveled for hours to a *hesder yeshiva*, a program which combines advanced Talmudic studies with military service, more than two hundred miles from our home. They traveled not only along the length of our nation, but also along the length of our souls; our child was moving on.

It is not so much that becoming an adult means giving up juvenile pleasures like play; adults make music, art, and theatre. We like to laugh. It is not so much that getting older means becoming overwrought with responsibilities; adults have more freedoms than do children. Rather, it is that during a transitional span, one passage ends in order for another one to open.

For the next five years, our older son will be focusing on learning Torah, serving in the Israeli Defense Force, and then focusing once more on learning Torah. Initially, his longest breaks will be three weeks in duration. Thereafter, it is likely that the largest blocks of time, during which he visits us, will be whichever handful of days surrounds his older sister's wedding. Those vacations will take place during the intermediate days of Sukkot, i.e., during the intermediate days of the Feast of Tabernacles, during the intermediate days of Passover, and during the summer. The wedding will take place when G-d approves the schedule.

Whereas our boy can always come home again, each time he retraces his route, we will be receiving a new young man. I believe that our beloved will remain the soft spoken, passionately loyal being that he was when he left our domain. I also believe that his depth of Torah and his experience of harsh realities will necessarily alter him.

He knows this truth, as do I. Both of us were in tears when he stepped beyond our family's threshold.

Mind you, this kid is no pushover. He knows the history and make of war machines of several lands. His imaginary creature of choice is a grown Komodo dragon. He is trained in mixed martial arts, and can, in a good eye, execute literally lethal moves. What's more, he plays bass (!)

And yet, this young man was raised in a home that values tenderness and respect, in a family that tries to respond to life's challenges with sensitivity, under the tutelage of parents who work to provide their children with consistent loving care. Thus, no one among us was surprised when our Torah student took to the road grieving his loss of certain physical and emotional safeties or when, upon watching him leave, I grieved my lost ability to shelter him.

It's not so much which schools this would-be scholar-warrior attended before moving out, what he earned on standardized tests or in classes before this nexus, or how much mastery he achieved in arts or sciences before he reached this level. That our cherished child formerly trashed his room by strewing his floor with piles of interlocking building materials, too, is of small relevance.

Unquestionably, my husband and I recall more than his childhood toys. We remember when he was an infant, him insisting on nursing when and as long as he wanted to nurse, We remember that when he was a toddler, he had angelic, white-blond hair. We remember his preschool needs to dig in the dirt and to play the music of trains on a carved flute. We remember, too, that in kindergarten, he liked math puzzles and made friends with all of his classmates.

For this young man, the one sent to the hills to learn Torah and combat, elementary school was all about *Navi*, Prophets, *Gemara* Club, and science experiments. "Free time" meant jumping from one staircase landing to another, without gripping banisters, and meant testing the structural limits of our century-old house.

By the time that this son hit adolescence, our family was on a plane heading for Israel. As a fairly new immigrant, he read his Bar Mitzvah Torah portion at the Kotel. Here, in the Old World, as was true there, in the New World, this son liked walking with his father to synagogue.

As per his siblings, he bonded with them, albeit in ways confounding to his parents. One sister, he tormented, just a little. Another he raced through books or along park avenues. His younger brother was almost always the recipient of pillow fights, "ninja" attacks and other expressions of his gentle affections.

Despite all of the above, the day arrived when he became taller than his father and a better chess player than his mother. High school graduation, too, came much too soon.

The intervening summer, the one between requisite education and *hesder*, was one of brooding, of reflecting, and of denial. The season of his childhood was not, in his mind, meant to end.

Nonetheless, this gunslinging Torah student chose a school a great distance from home, knowing in the secret wisdom of his soul that the rabbis there would become his allies in elevation, and that the other young men there would become his lifetime friends. He chose well.

Before Older Dude left our home, he asked me to speak to him not of our shared past, not of our probable futures, and not of our mutual imaginary friends, but of the present. I had little to offer. My deep inhalations and exhalations were all I could summon; we were sending him into the world young and expecting him to return fully fledged.

He hugged me, anyway. My maternal heart washed with loss and hope. I imagine his filial heart filled with the same.

Becoming a Participant in National Service

My past few Tuesdays have looked something like this:

6:30: get up.

6:45: get out of bed.

6:50: dump contents of closet on the floor while trying to find an outfit.

6:55: put on the first outfit I took out.

7:00-7:15: wonder why I lack time to get ready for school when I wake up at 6:30.

8:00: arrive at school.

8:30-4:00: learn, or at least sit in class and draw pictures.

4:10: leave school and start walking towards my bus stop.

4:13: remember that the bus stop was moved, get annoyed at "the stupid bus people," turn around, and then go to my new bus stop.

5:00: get home, throw my backpack in my room, and search the fridge for food.

5:05: open the fridge again, hoping that something new appeared there in the last five minutes.

5:10: empty fridge dregs for making stir fry.

5:11: add another two onions and a second red pepper 'cause everyone else will want some.

5:55: log onto the National Service, *Sherut Leumi,* website and have hand poised to click the button to sign up for an interview the second the registration opens, at 6:00.

6:00.25: *Sherut Leumi* net crashes; everyone else had the same idea as I did.

For me, *Sherut Leumi,* or even finishing high school, used to seem like a faraway moment. They were events I knew were coming, but they seemed so distant that I never thought a lot about them. Then, suddenly, I am in the midst of *Sherut Leumi* interviews; I'm signing up for interviews, searching for button down shirts five minutes before my bus comes, and missing tests because I am trying to convince people that I'm are the best person for their jobs.

It's not a simple process, but luckily the government (I think it's the government) is helping us high school seniors out. Representatives from the three *Sherut Leumi* organizations came to talk to us about various *Sherut Leumi* places. They gave us pamphlets and told us to call with questions, too.

I made my pamphlet into origami. I tried to call a representative, but every time I called I was sent to voice mail. My parents have no idea what's going on. I've been left pretty much on my own, which is basically fine.

I managed to sign up for three different places, and even got to those places' interviews on time. Each place is very different from the other two, as were their respective interviews. At one place, I gave a presentation and put on a play. At another, I wrote an essay about my role model and told them that I am *definitely* a people person. At my third interview, just a few days ago, during a time when I had a fever and about two hours of sleep (our senior play was the night before), I think I managed to convince them that I was adept with computers and that I *love, love, love* what their organization does, but I'm not sure; that day was sort of a haze.

Until I get my results though, I'm taking a break from thinking about *Sherut Leumi* and am focusing on Purim. I'm certain that everything will work out well. Next year will be lots of fun, and as soon as I know where I will be serving as a *Bat Shirut*, a daughter of service, I can start stressing out about my next big milestone, *psychometrics*, secondary education mastery exams.

— Rivka

"Absorption," in a word, is a process. When our family was blessed to make immigration to Israel, my husband and I anticipated the linguistic and cultural shock we would experience due to our family being transplanted from North America to the Middle East. We also anticipated feeling impotent due to our children, Bless G-d, getting the chance to grow up in a social milieu unlike any that we, ourselves, had known. We were wrong; the term "shock" is an inadequate description for the wrenching of our guts with which my husband and I, as parents of immigrants, have become familiar.

It's understandable that my husband and I were ill-prepared for our children to return home from school with stories about friends' siblings having been killed or mutilated by war by merely walking through

Jerusalem. It's reasonable that we had no seasoned response to our kids' tales of intolerance among Jews. Also, it's explicable that Computer Cowboy and I were without resources for helping our offspring sort through this country's bureaucrats' rhetoric about poverty rates and about other aberrations of social decency.

Consider that our family was blessed, in a good eye: to have arrived in this Holy Land at a dynamic time, to live among our tribes, and to dwell in the most awesome of cities, Jerusalem. We also knew that we were moving here at the beginning, perhaps, of the social pains marking the coming of *Moshiach*, the messiah.

What we failed to appreciate, though, was that the professionalism, the integrity, and many other of the hallmarks of human interaction, which we took for granted when we lived in the New World, would be palpably missing here. About those differences in quality of life, my husband and I remain without words.

There are further dissimilarities, for which we were ill-prepared, as well. The New World's flavor of "Yeshivish" is hardly the Old World's flavor of "Charadei." Those, among our kids, who might have opted for a black hat in the States, are happy prancing about in Israel with knit yarmulkes and short payot. Yesterday's Bayit Yaakov girl is today's Rav Kook school attendee. In addition, those little ones, who used to live in a home where "glatt" was good enough, now find themselves in a home where even kashrut is more selective. Nuances play differently in Israel than elsewhere.

And yet, all of the aforementioned distinctions in shades of meaning are but a part of the influences that impacted my family when we arrived at this nexus. Our choices for schools, for synagogues, and for others of our associations are not the choices we might have made in our former home. Here, our friends, both religious and secular, are a bit more to the right than they were in the New World, and our family's level of tolerance is a bit more to the left than it used to be.

Our aspirations for our children's spouses and careers are no longer the aspirations of well-educated middle class Americans, but of struggling, grateful, middle class Israelis. *Hesder yeshivot* are in our boys' futures. *Shirut Leumi* is slated for our girls. Trying to place our kids in competitive universities that feature a Hillel or Chabad or other sources for kosher food and friends is moot; Israel is Jewish and the kids will, with the help of

Heaven, likely be married long before they finish their undergraduate studies.

Facets of life, which are immaterial in the New World, matter a lot in this Old World. Here, the year(s) immediately following high school graduation is/are not about placement in Greek organizations or in honors programs, but about getting significant and useful life experiences and about giving one's best efforts to one's country. To wit, the first baby that Computer Cowboy and I were blessed to have, Missy Older, has been interviewing for her National Service position.

That bright kid has been told her Hebrew's "not good enough" for all sorts of encounters. She's been told, simultaneously, that her extracurricular experiences and others of her accomplishments surpass the thresholds otherwise established. In other words, she's an Israeli with ordinary civic duties, but she's not an ordinary Israeli.

In the end, our child interviewed for positions that will allow her to use her English in tandem with her Hebrew. She offered herself to an organization that teaches tourists about The Temple, to an organization that eases the way for new immigrants, and to an organization that specializes in outreach. In the weeks to come, we'll hear about whom, among those agencies, appreciates her skills, talents, energy and faith.

Regardless of where she lands, Missy Older will be the first among our children to walk where her parents never footed. We can support, but not guide her. My husband and I feel our innards tumbling all over again.

— Hannah

Talking Fish, Fidgety Parrots, and the Rest of the Menagerie

When I appreciate familial events through the lenses of talking fish, of fidgety parrots, or of other members of the local menagerie, I experience enjoyment. When I don't, in contrast, I feel put upon. At this point in my life, it serves me well to choose the more upbeat of those ways of regarding near relatives' passages.

More specifically, as my children and I age, I feel increasingly confounded by them. At present, all of my sons and daughters are adolescents or are older. I struggle to ride out the waves of their exuberance and of their other related, but not necessarily sunshiny, albeit communicated feelings. To wit, I gain no end of utility whenever I smile and nod, rather than act in kind, in response to my kids' antics. After all, those children have embarked on the vital process of differentiation. Their pushing at boundaries means they are living healthfully.

I don't have to resort to shouting merely because all of the residents of my home try to get out the door, to school, and to work, at once, while "forgetting" about the dishes in the sink, the toilet lids at full mast, or the questionably clean laundry on the staircase. Such happenings remain insufficient reason for me to sit on the sofa and cry.

Just as chronicling Martian uprisings will do nothing to stymie Earthly social movements, just as liberating pound puppies will not at all help the victims of domestic abuse, and just as protesting slave-waged piece work, while insisting on buying only the cheapest of produced goods will forever neglect marketplace causality, so, too will jumping up and down or performing some other parental gymnastics not yield improved results when my kids act childish. Those teens and twenties could not care less if I pout or screech.

On the other hands, little cogs, when not turning big wheels, can be harnessed to motors, which, in turn, can "drive the family car." Said differently, teen energy can be well employed; it can be redirected toward fruitful ends.

For instance, when a recently visiting young gal, here in the Holy Land for a year, sighed over not being able to make kugel or challah during her seminary stint, I invited her to invade, that is, to make use of, my family's kitchen. The result of that change in course, from complaining to creating, is that she's due to arrive for a "cooking party" this Thursday.

To boot, other, older visitors to our home, on immigration to Israel without benefit of immediate family, young women who lamented, aloud, their lack of a local Jewish mother and their lack of access to a functional sushi mat, too, are due in our home on Thursday. I "agreed" on their making fried rice, too.

In another example, a dear son-of-the-heart, the one who drifted through our home last week and stayed long enough to learn, from my older son, how to make olive dip, similarly is scheduled to make an appearance in our domicile that day. That particular twenty-something asked to taste the sushi that's getting made by the girls and asked to graduate to mashing tomatoes.

Soup's up. Even with all the sampling and "take home prizes," I hope to glean some elements of our three Sabbath meals and to give a variety of emerging adults a sense of accomplishment. I don't cook using recipes and neither does anyone passing through my kitchen. The guys and gals, who will be here, are in for some imagination and fun.

My new son-in-law, who started out here chopping salads, late one night before the wedding canopy, is scheduled to move up to soup during that same day. I envisioned egg drop, to go along with the eastern dishes, but, as reported my older daughter, that son-in-law's wife, he would rather dice chicken.

No complaints. Chicken soup? Check! Challot? Check! Kugel? Check! Sushi? Unlikely to have any left. Fried rice? Check! Salads? Check! Our kugelmaker, meanwhile, crooned on about her need to create. I have no intention of stopping her. Party on!

Along those lines, recently, when my younger son had lots of extra energy, I sent him to our rooftop sunporch to weed. During that same span, when my married daughter passed through and remarked how much she missed engaging in home maintenance (beginner apartments only have a few square feet of living space). I pointed her to her father's toolbox, to a semi-clogged drain, and to a closet that needed to be disassembled.

When my older son sighed over hanging up his nicest Sabbath shirts outside in the rain (those bits of clothing have yet to be proven to be dryer safe), I told him to bring in a portable rack. I returned to my office. A few weeks short of twenty, that kid managed to figure out what to do. Likewise, my younger daughter, the one who wanted to redecorate her room, got greenlit. Her end result, a grand display of postcards on her walls, cost nothing but clear tape and her endeavor gave her a new sense of mastery.

During another period, when one of the lights of my life thought she could engender my good graces by making me tea, I requested fennel. When her sibling offered to rub their dad's bedraggled, just-returned-from-work back for five minutes, I suggested he do so for ten. There's not much wrong, and a whole bunch right, in shepherding kids' resources toward familial benefit.

Consequently, I plan to continue to encourage alien costume balls, sea creature-friendly outdoor markets, and intelligent broadcasts of alternate mopping and sweeping arrangements. Except for members of select political groups, most of the young folks with whom I interact, both those to the manor born, and those whom are borrowed, view my invitations to get creative as benign, at worst, intriguing, at best.

As long as my juveniles act "delinquent," I will endeavor to imagine cups of hot sip, kind words, and other sorts of finite goodness. Even if I have to go on picking up errant socks, refilling the toilet paper holder, and ignoring the rainbow-hued mold growing on select items in the fridge, I will consider myself blessed.

Torah Teachers and Other Treasures

Recently, my family had the honor of serving coffee in our home, here, in Israel, to the rabbi and rebbetzin who built the bridge that brought us from the secular life to the religious one. That dear couple was visiting The Holy Land for a celebration. Their arrival in Israel meant an additional festivity for my family.

A decade and change ago, my family knew our essential selves to be Jewish, but had no idea what present depth or grand history such a heritage could call forward. The appellation "Jewish" seemed, back then, no more of a special sort of nomenclature than did the word "red," in the service of describing apples, or "hot," as used to refer to the kind of weather one might experience in August.

We were clueless that we could choose to open ourselves to a texture of life richer than anything built from finance or from fickle social status. Up until the point at which my husband and I made a commitment to learn about Torah living, our days and nights, like those of the other people in our circle, were largely measured by who we knew, what we accomplished, and the like.

Fortunately, a series of life and death events, which smacked us upside the head, forced us to heed the types of goings-on that we otherwise conveniently ignored. Working on character traits takes effort. That effort, in turn, initially, often hurts.

With a smile, those leaders, a young couple who did not even reside in the same town as the minyan over which they presided, schlepped their pots and pans, their *seforim*, their foodstuffs, their candles, their kosher wine, their homemade challot, and their children, so that suburban Jewish souls might have a taste of a better life. They did not chide us or our fellow learners for our ignorance, electing instead to focus on helping us become accountable for our time on this world.

Erroneously, we, and people like us, assumed, at first, that if we didn't instantly transform into someones who resembled our teachers, we would never morph. It had been our experience, in the business world, in academia, and in additional positions of secular leadership, that the best view was from the top. It had been our experience that the top was a seat large enough for only a few or, maybe, for only a single individual. It had been our experience that any and all means of acquiring that most superlative position were justified by the desired end.

What we learned under the rabbi and rebbetzin's tutelage, however, was that growth: is personal, is beyond the strictures of mundane paradigms, and is available to all Jews, simultaneously. We were encouraged to integrate foreign ideas such as "slowing down" and such as "not competing." Our guides were liberating us in significant ways.

In addition, at their table, we supped, sweetly, not just on Sabbath cholent or on Purim cakes, but also on the concept that individual development, in isolation from the healing of the collective, is relatively worthless. More practically, anyone among us, who merit knowing a little about Torah, is at once obliged to give that knowledge over to other people. Our former model of the hasty, self-serving catapult was emptying of meaning. From the rabbi and his rebbetzin, we learned to respect ourselves and then to respect others, in ways, which prior, we had never given credence.

Modesty, for instance, we learned, was not about antiquated modes of dressing, but about separating the private from public view; "Kashrut," likewise, we discovered, was about bestowing holiness on eating and drinking, not about some ill-advised martyrdom involving reading the fine print on labels. "Learning Torah" was about acquiring a blueprint for living, not about one-upping the kid in the next row by reciting, but not understanding, words and ideas. We lost interest in self-promotion and gained interest in reaching closer to The Name. Our best moments became constituted by deeds of loving kindness, which we merited to also comprehend.

Concurrently, we taught our children how to cross the street, inspected hand-me-down clothes for rips and tears before passing them on to others of our offspring, burned the soup, forgot socks in the laundry pile, and buried, after they had lived out their lives, various pets. We carpooled, we paid taxes, we stepped in national rallies, we picked up litter, we ran away from seemingly rabid squirrels, and we anchored our jungle gyms again and again, so that our children and our neighbors' children would remain safe even when pumping the swings too high.

Our rabbi and rebbetzin did not rush us or any of their other students away from our insular yuppie lives. As a result, we were able, Bless G-d, to "climb the mountain" without having to turn back due to the "altitude poisoning," which can result from moving too high, too fast. Later, when we learned that would-be hikers before us had failed from their bursts of short-lived enthusiasm, and later still, when we learned that there really is no peak to reach, no summit to attain, just more and more years of marching forward, we were grateful for the wisdom of the rabbi and rebbetzin who held us back until we learned to pace ourselves.

We were grateful for their closed-mouth encouragement, too. No one laughed at my ill-fated first wig. No one criticized my husband's first pronunciation of kiddush. No one scolded our young children for not having longer pants or skirts or sleeves.

These many years later, those babies and elementary school kids, whom we brought with us to the rabbi and rebbetzin's home, have grown and are ready to set up households of their own. These many years later, the rebbetzin looks a little more tired and the rabbi looks a little more gray. At the same time, the rebbetzin seems a little more radiant and the rabbi seems a little more luminous. They are still building connections, for Jews, from the world of illusions to the world of truth. We, their spiritual children, are right behind them, filling up pails with holy bricks and of sacred mortar.

Educational Assets

While cleaning out my office, I came across notes taken at an education workshop for pre-immigration to Israel. To say that "I was wowed" by my finding would be analogous to saying that "Jerusalem is a reasonable destination for a religious Jew."

At the time, my transliteration of Hebrew phrases was nothing if not funny. My Hebrew, then, was pathetic, "worse than unintelligible," only changing, post immigration, to "incoherent," and, just recently, improving to "extremely deficient." I dream of elevating my Hebrew to "mediocre," and eventually, to "adequate." Not only was I unable to spell words such as "*bagrut*," "matriculation exam," but I had no clue about the nature of such exams, let alone about the nature of psychometrics or of other important high school tests.

My pre-immigration to Israel jottings showed me to be pretty clueless, as well, about the worldview delineations in Israeli schools. Whereas the New World's sometimes slim differences between "modern" and "Yeshivish" schools challenged me; the Israeli variations, among Torah institutions, more than flummoxed me. My workshop notebook proffered multicolored diagrams underscoring my bafflement about the degrees of difference among "Dati," "Dati Torani," "Chardali," and "Charadei," and demonstrated how Israeli "Dati Torani" is New World "modern," but Israeli "Chardali," not Israeli "Charadei," is New World "Yeshivish."

The educational consultants to whom I spoke that night further exacerbated my confusion; they offered, Israeli-style, conflicting opinions as to where my kids ought to wind up. In the end, one child went to a Lubavitch school and then to a hesder-type school, one went to a Dati Torani school, and two went to Rav Kook schools reputed for their "*Mitzrachi*," eastern, nature. The kids' Israeli enrollments mystified my Old World friends more than they mystified Computer Cowboy and me. Yet, those same friends eat at our table, where guests might be associated with: Breslov, Mir Yeshiva, Beer Sheva Medical School, Bait Yaakov seminaries, "exploratory" seminaries, Tzfardi minyanim, Holland, Africa, Russia, or nonreligious New World neighborhoods.

Placement was but one of my pre-immigration confusions. Notwithstanding my social science training, I could barely parse the data on Israeli teachers. I obediently wrote down the concepts, but failed to understand how: staging sit-ins in school offices wouldn't "black list" my family, calling teachers at home wouldn't create resentment, and arranging lots of meetings wouldn't waste teacher and parent time.

Spending a short season on the ground, though, changed my view. Israeli education is not about docile children sitting in well-funded houses of learning, while excitedly inhaling Torah (if one of those variables is at work in your child's school, say prayers of gratitude. If two are present, rehearse your child to shut his/her mouth; you've discovered a rare phenomenon to be shared only with people to whom you owe *protexia*, the act of looking out exclusively for "one's own." If all three variables are existent, check your kidney stone medication; you are hallucinating).

Israeli education is plagued by overcrowded, under-funded classrooms, and by a dearth of ordinary equipment, supplies, and books. Here, parents buy texts for their children when they can locate those texts. Once, I gave up on a book search; the proprietors of Jerusalem's shops were unwilling to order even one additional copy of a math book that Missy Younger needed. Consequently, Missy Younger shared her friends' copies or did without.

Further, Israeli kids are tense (they may also be "intense," but posturing is the prerogative of all teens). My kids' classmates' siblings have been blown up, or "merely lightly injured," defending our homeland. My kids' classmates have attended long days of school on empty stomachs. My kids' classmates have accepted that their teachers will disappear for a day, a week, or a month, without a replacement, school budgets being what they are, when those teachers are on maternity leave, fulfilling reserve duty, or busy with an emergency involving their own children.

Most Israeli kids will never have the: mandatory violin lessons, free afterschool European languages programs, a plethora of sports enrichment opportunities, computer labs, parents volunteering as docents for school districts' displays of investment art, high-tech playgrounds, individualized reading and composition instruction, or better-than-municipal-library book collections, enjoyed by pupils in some New World public schools. What's more, most Israeli kids will also never experience the "extras" of New

World Torah schools, such as: clean interiors, working bathrooms, and regular schedules.

In the New World, teachers do not have to weigh purchasing study aids against feeding their own children. In the New World, few kids get physically battered by classmates ("the preferred" New World method of peer torture is psychological assault. In the New World, I could assuage psychological hurt. Here, I was only able to pray gratitude that newbie Younger Dude and newbie Older Dude got beat up on the same day, when we first moved in). Yet, New World schools lack an important fundamental of Israeli education; New World schools lack "we." New World schools offer only "us" and "them."

Teachers not only provide their home phone numbers, but also call to see if all is okay when a child is sick for more than a day. Here, as well, teachers network with tutors and then announce, *a fait compli*, that they have solved the educational problems beleaguering their students' parents.

Here, kids roll all over each other, like a tangle of lizards, to share photos of new nieces or nephews, to be the first in line to give names for their classes' *Psalms* lists, and to share lunch with someone who has none. Here, the school holidays are our holidays. Here, despite the fact that lice are communal, so, too, are festivities (I draw the line, however, at thirty little girls exploring all of our closets and drawers; Missy Younger might have to have her Bat Mitzvah celebration in a public park).

In the New World, teen "visits" are the formal stuff of phone calls, and of checking and of rechecking Facebook. Here, I caution Missy Older's best friend to hitch safely and I listen attentively as Older Dude's friends' share their plans for nighttime (!) travel home at the same time as they are rambling on about their older brothers' acquisition of gun licenses.

Here, if Missy Younger gives me contact information and parents' names, requests permission, and assures me that she has packed her cell phone, her bus money, and clean underwear, Missy Younger may sleep among piles of girls whose homes I have never visited. Here, she brings home sweet daughters of rabbis, of scientists, of butchers, and of cab drivers, all of whose parents I have never met.

Here, Younger Dude runs to play with his neighborhood friend and with that friend's five siblings, in a home where Younger Dude can jabber forever in contemporary Hebrew without being considered an extra source of noise. Here, more small visitors are no problem.

After I thought about the Old World and New World education systems, I balled up those pre-immigration notes. That workshop's ideas were dated. Mostly, my children's Israeli, educational successes derive from the warmth of their classmates and from the warmth of their teachers. It is fortunate that they are growing up here.

Learning Partners

On Passover, The Jewish people merits, Bless G-d, to say "*dayenu*," "enough," i.e., The Boss showers us with an abundance of kindnesses. As individuals, we can say the same. A case in point, is the group of wonderful first teachers with whom I had been blessed.

In 1998, our youngest child, following a gestation full of prayers and hardships (sixteen emergency trips to hospitals and other assorted "challenges" counted among our tests), joined us in this world. Whereas one cannot bargain with The Master of the Universe, one can make requests and one can make promises.

I promised, in thanks, after my child was born, in a good eye, alive and healthy, two distinct miracles, that we would give him the traditional first haircut and that we would get him to a *yeshiva*. I had no idea what I was promising, only that my family had been granted great compassion, that I wanted to express my appreciation to The Boss, and that acting in a "religious" manner, as my limited understanding defined that concept, might count as a pittance of actualized repayment.

Keep in mind, The Highest One has plans to which none of us are privy. He Sees the entire painting whereas, if sagacious, we might perceive one of Creation's smaller splotches. One fraction of a dot of a tiny area of that pigmentation, which constitutes the life of the Greenberg Family, was G-d linking us to a rabbi associated with an individualized learning situation long before our miracle baby was born.

More specifically, the Source of Cosmic Compassion put my family in touch with a tolerant, "local orthodox rabbi." We sought such a guide because the religious leaders, whom we already knew, were not giving us words that hit us in our deepest places. Matters of life and death call for reaching simultaneously into the lowest points and toward the greatest heights.

That today my family consists of Torah Jews testifies to the many bridges that our newfound rabbi and his rebbetzin built for us. At the time, their reluctance to cast judgment and their authentically offered shepherding enabled us to change our kitchen, to upgrade our manner of praying (we ultimately joined their congregation), and to begin to explore the sorts of Torah education that were regionally available for our children. In addition, that rabbi and rebbetzin helped our family connect with an adult learning program.

My first partner was a young, Bait Yaakov assistant teacher, who harkened from Lakewood. Weekly, we met face-to-face. She and a few of her young friends schlepped from their community to ours. Our new rabbi's congregation was growing.

With that wonderful young lady, I rehearsed the rudiments of being observant. I learned about covering my hair, about giving *shaliach manot*, food baskets, on Purim, and about not singing in front of men or reaching beyond the gender-separating partition to kiss the Torah during services. My partner illuminated how to live an observant life.

Today, Bless G-d, that lovely lady's husband learns in *kollel*, an institute for the full-time, advanced study of Talmud and rabbinic literature, and her children learn in *chedarrim*, schools in which Hebrew and religious knowledge are taught. Her first adult student, me, learns in Jerusalem.

After the young lady, I was partnered with a grandmom. My questions about family purity and about similar subjects were awkward for my initial instructor at the time, who was a single woman just out of seminary. Although sometimes, I spoke about such matters with that twenty-something's mother, who herself was a pleasant and knowledgeable woman, her mom's calendar was already filled with regular, community-based deeds of loving kindness and as such made her mom an unlikely candidate to help with my continued growth. I needed to find an escort: whose demographics were closely matched to mine, who had some time, and who participated in the same learning program as me.

With my first partner's approval, I switched to a middle-aged study partner from Borough Park. At least weekly, over the phone, my second teacher and I explored likely paths for me to take in my pursuit of becoming a more observant midlife mother and wife. With her, I learned about domestic harmony and about working with yeshiva and day school teachers to insure that my children's education suited them.

That second partner brought me to my first Agudah Convention. She included my family at her family's celebrations. I met her generations.

She was as successful as my first partner was at bringing me to a new level. My husband and I, with our newfound local orthodox rabbi's blessings, moved from our secular community to an observant one. Our children enrolled in religious schools. To wit, my husband and I devoted ourselves to a life of Torah and good deeds.

Shortly thereafter, with my second partner's okay, I took on yet a newer partner, a local woman with whom I could sit, chair to chair, to learn the weekly Torah portion.

Like my teachers who preceded her, that wonderful friend elevated me to new levels of understanding. She also taught me how to blend a delicious fruit soup and how to make any visitor to my home feel important.

My family would not have gotten far along the Torah path and would not have progressed so quickly if we had not been gifted with the generosity of our early teachers. My experiences, in this regard, make it easy for me to understand why we Jews give honor to all of our educators and not just to the ones who walk us through intermediate or advanced learning. Without primary resources, it would be impossible to approach further enrichments.

A few years passed, after which The Name brought my family to Israel. His Kindnesses are unending. There are no express elevators to becoming more observant; there are only stairs, per se, to take us upward.

Individualized learning was a profound step for us. While it would have been enough if our baby had been born alive, while it would have been enough if our baby had also been born healthy, while it would have been enough had The Almighty revealed to us the value of an observant life, and while it would have been enough had The Infinite arranged for us to meet a wise, local orthodox rabbi, generously, The Boss also gave us people with whom to learn His Torah. Dayenu!

"Ephraim" and "Manasseh"

It's a pity that most folk, Yours Truly included, don't really grasp how to perform deeds of loving kindness toward other people. Recently, while enjoying a salad at a local cafe, I merited witnessing the actions of someone who had mastered that way of living. That Jew seemed to be engaging in acts of loving kindness for The Name's sake, not for his own personal gain.

Specifically, the Jew on view, whom I'll call "Manasseh," enacted continuous, unexaggerated, humble consideration to another Jew, whom I'll call "Ephraim." Ephraim, you see, was troubled by some kind of cognitive difference.

Ephraim, despite sitting in a public eatery, and despite being somewhere past middle age, called out, whistled, smacked his own face loudly, and so forth. Nonetheless, Manasseh did not respond to his buddy, but, instead engaged him. That is, Manasseh did not react, but chose to participate proactively, chose to communicate with his associate in a way that is typical of dining with friends or with family members. Manasseh proffered no jarred movements or articulations, did not hesitate when it was his turn in conversation, and made no sour faces.

Perhaps Ephraim had been Manasseh's learning partner for decades, and had had, as of late, a stroke or other incapacitating experience. In that case, Manasseh was treating his dear one as the valuable soul, which he long knew his dear one to be. Alternatively, perhaps Ephraim was a relative of Manasseh's, a brother, an uncle, or a cousin, whom Manasseh cherished all of his years despite Moshe's apparent trials. Maybe, Ephraim was a neighbor, a member of a community house of prayer, or some other nonfamilial relation to Manasseh. Then again, perhaps, Ephraim was a gifted scholar with a speech impediment and with other hardships.

I will never know those men's connection. I do not need to. I need only to be aware that Manasseh's interpersonal communication was as matter of fact to him as was the way in which he spread his butter on his bread and as was the way in which he sipped his seltzer. His tone of voice was neither patronizing nor impatient. His interactions were remarkable *because* they were not noteworthy. Specifically, he treated his companion as most of us would treat folks who were not similarly distressed.

After the men said "Grace after Meals," they left the shop. On their way out, Ephraim continued to gesture and to sound off in his seemingly random way. Manasseh continued to talk to his associate about the sorts of things about which most people speak; the weather, the upcoming holiday of Chanukah, a bit of the weekly Torah portion, and a nearby shop's sale on socks.

I believe that Ephraim, either cognitively, or somewhere deeper in his soul, depending on the specific nature of his inner difference, knows and appreciates that Manasseh treats him like a person of integrity and honor. I believe that Manasseh values Ephraim. I am grateful for both of them.

As I finished my cucumbers and radishes, I thought about what I had been blessed to behold. I reflected, as well, on my own inability to be inconspicuously considerate to individuals whose public presence differs from mine.

Too often, I am gracious only when it is easy to do so. Saying "yes" to a request when I am rested is far easier than is saying "yes" when I am fatigued. Likewise, too often, I offer up compassion when I have time or am in the right mood. Providing emotional sustenance for others when I am "high" from life feels as though it takes fewer resources than does providing emotional sustenance for others when I am encumbered. In the same way, benevolence, whose "benefits" are known to me, appears less complicated than does benevolence whose "benefits" are known only to The Name.

Apart from my level of development in the area of extending honor toward others, I received a gift when observing Ephraim and Manasseh interrelate. My erudition came from noting Manasseh's unaffected respect for his cohort. My education came, as well, from seeing Ephraim's regard of their outing as normal and from seeing him consider his breakfast partner's thoughtfulness as *de rigueur*.

The Name created each and every one of our souls. Sadly, it still takes a "big" person to communicate in a way that disregards those small, truly unimportant differences that all of us harbor and it takes an even bigger person to overlook the irregularities extended toward him in making social meaning. In my esteem, Manasseh is a giant from whom I must learn. Yet, Ephraim, whose footprint is even more amazing, too, is my teacher.

Supernal Music

May our eyes see your return to Zion with love.
The one who restores his presence to Zion.

The above phrases begin Naftali Kalfa's newest song, "Zion," which is part of a larger project undertaken in collaboration with Shlomo Katz, and with other fantastic singers and instrumentalists. This composition's very existence, as well as its masterful beckoning, illuminates humanity's fundamental ability to connect with The Holy One, Blessed be He, through music joined with words.

Although all of creation praises The Name in song, it is humanity to whom The Boss has granted the ability to add language. Perhaps one reason for this great gift is to provide us with light in times of darkness. In His infinite kindness, The Master of the Universe created a form of communication compelling enough to lift our souls up from the deeply stuck places in this world and to aim us toward The World to Come. Most people, fortunately, have repeatedly experienced this rise.

No matter the degree of proficiency or of practicality in any of our individual tunes, all such spiritually-infused expressions can pull us and others away from hopelessness to the possibility of return and to the probabilities of faith and trust. The nature of "ordinary" combinations of sound is, after all, to produce beauty via form, harmony, and emotional truth.

Relatively speaking, voices gilded by The Boss brighten us that much more. Heavenly-impacted human reverberations enable us to think, to feel, and to act as an elevated people, as a community intent on cobbling lives out of consecutive instances of honoring The Name.

Naftali Kalfa is one such aureate of musical excellence empowered to lead us along that desired route. He looks to Torah to increase the spiritual splendor of our world, claiming that, "religion is an essential part of what defines you and who you are. Everything you do artistically or otherwise comes from that same vessel whose essence is based upon religion."[1] In other words, Kalfa grasps that not only does music's quality affect the people that it enthuses, but that musicians' values, too, impact strongly upon their audiences.

It follows that our better character traits are awakened by Kalfa's recordings. I cry in joy, awe, anticipation, and belonging every time I listen to "Zion."

As a modest Jew, one who strives not for riches and fame, but to serve The Almighty, to advance the Jewish People, and to bring *Moshiach*, the messiah, now, Reb Kalfa successfully removes spiritual blockages by dint of his songs. Humble Mr. Kalfa's tunes shine through his "constantly striv[ing] to connect to higher worlds, worlds which do not involve … finite mediators. [He] believes[s] that music speaks to and touches our souls in ways that words never can."[2] He is right. He correctly assesses that "deep down inside every Jewish essence, our souls are all yearning to connect the way we did in the Temple, which was always through song."[3]

Yet, he would sooner laud his wife and praise his children than highlight his gift, in a good eye. Kalfa sees himself as learning from all people, including from his "youngest daughter, Eden, who cannot yet speak[. W]hen she connects to specific songs, [he learns] from [his] baby the power of music to connect in ways that words never can."[4]

May you build it up in our days as an everlasting sanctuary.
And prepare the throne of David your servant.

Whereas Naftali made immigration to Israel from Toronto, no matter where he's lived, "music has always been in [his] soul. From a very young age, [he] would sing in synagogues and for community events. [Naftali's] musical talent and inclination come from [his] mother, who is a talented singer and musician, who plays both flute and guitar."[5] His artistry has been influenced, as well, by many greats, including: Shlomo Carlebach, Avraham Fried, and Mordechai Ben David. Beyond his immediate family and the aforementioned great artists, Naftali Kalfa has drawn inspiration from his countrymen, from individuals who have "encouraged and inspired [him] to pursue [his] dreams and ambitions, irrelevant of the likelihood of success or the absurdness of the challenge."[6] Some folks "never get in touch with [their creativity] or develop it[, but Kalfa has long considered his art to be about] creativity, and how we use [it] with God's help."[7]

True, Kalfa seeks first to be "a good Jew, father, husband, son, and friend….to maximize his potential as a human being."[8] Nonetheless, his talent is recognized so extensively that he works with musicians of the caliber of Gad Elbaz, of "Shyne" and of Yossi Piamenta. His Kalfa's first musical production, "Yihyu Liratzon" was fashioned with the Piamenta Brothers.

In addition, while the array of the music that he embraces (contrast, for example, Kalfa's "Vaani Tefilati" with his "Zion") necessitates that he takes artistic risks, he does not let himself sink into worry; "With any art or music, there will always be people who love it and people that hate it. I make music that touches me and excites me. If the public enjoys it, that is a bonus. As long as I make my family proud and I am not creating art that I don't connect to, I am very content."[9]

Despite his art's strength to bring people higher, Kalfa would still love to be able to walk all of his audiences through his work. He wishes he could "sit down with every person before they listen to or watch [any of his] song[s], and tell them the background of the song, how and where it was created and what inspired it, so that when they experience it, they know how it came into being."[10] Authentic caring is one dimension of Kalfa's genius.

With so much of our world left for us to repair, before we can herald the advent of *Moshiach*, we are fortunate to be able to take up the music of Naftali Kalfa. His endowment can help carry us through our most essential work.

> *May the Temple be built and the City of Zion filled.*
> *And there we will sing a new song, and with joy ascend.*

The Death of a Dear Friend

Ecclesiastes says that there is a time for everything. There's a time to plant and a time to reap, a time to talk and a time not to talk, a time to be born, and a time to die.

Somehow, there seems to be no right time for death.

I don't know if I'll ever be able to accept death for what it is; the end of life. It's surreal for me to bury a friend and to think that I will never see him again. But I have to accept death and move on.

Recently, I heard a speech from a rabbi. This rabbi offered that the week of shiva is not an end, but rather a beginning and that the shiva week helps the family move on. I suppose that we must find the happiness in everything and keep that happiness when things seem hard.

The Nine Days, the time when we mourn the loss of the Temple, just ended. It was a sad time for me, but I don't feel that I mourned properly. I never had the Temple to lose, and thus was unable to feel the loss. I didn't know what I was missing.

Losing a friend is different. A friend is someone you know and care about. You feel you are missing a friend when the friend is not there. A friend is someone who, when you stand at his grave, even though the levayah pronounced his name, and even though you, yourself, heard the eulogies, you can't accept that you won't see him again.

Amongst all my mourning, I try to remind myself that I have no need to cry. I will see him tomorrow; *Moshiach*, the messiah, is coming!

— Rivka

Last night, a dear friend called. She didn't sound very good. I wondered if there was a new dynamic with her children (she certainly had heard about some of my family's ups and downs), with her or her husband's employment status (she had been privy to part of our saga), with her house hunt, or with some other important item. I didn't anticipate the subject of her call.

As her voice quaked, she told me to sit. Then she pronounced "Baruch Dayan Emet," "Bless the True Judge." Thereafter, she gently informed me that a mutual friend had been taken to the next realm.

This friend was in our age group. Our children are his children's peers. His wife is one of my loved others. Our homes have been open to each other on Sabbath, on holidays, and on ordinary afternoons.

We had just collectively celebrated Yom Ha'atzmaut, Independence Day. He had grilled treats for all of us. He had made sure there were comfortable chairs and enough food and drink for all comers. He had made necessary introductions. He had led us in an evening of Torah speeches.

This man was neither stranger nor casual acquaintance. He used to sit next to Older Dude during services. He and my husband, Computer Cowboy, used to walk home together, regularly, on Sabbaths, after synagogue.

He used to help my husband, for festivities, secure and haul tables and chairs from the local gemach. Only a good friend bothers getting sweaty, after a full day of work, for something as unglamorous as moving folded furniture.

This dear one was a learned fellow, a rabbi, in fact, though he didn't advertise his knowledge. Fortunate were the folk who shared a meal with him and heard his Torah. "By day," though, he worked in a humble vocation. He worked so that his family's absorption process could be successful. He loved his family. He loved Eretz Yisrael.

The levayah will take place shortly. The pain will linger. I cannot imagine the feelings in his wife's heart or in the souls of his daughters. My family and the other families who love this family will try, imperfectly, to support these friends.

The loss will go beyond the burial, beyond the week of *shiva*, beyond the thirty day period of *shloashim*. Each holiday without this father/husband, each season, each engagement, each wedding and each birth, will all be inflected with the whisper of loss.

— Hannah

80

Remembering Jeff Zaslow

Literally, many decades ago, when Computer Cowboy and I were college kids, we had a wonderful friend, Jeff Zaslow. That fellow Jewish writer had the prettiest sweethearts, the warmest roommates, and the best accolades from our teachers. He received those social merits because he, himself, was a fabulous human being.

Jeff didn't compete; he coordinated. He was not mean spirited, but was full of spirit. Remarkably, his vigor derived, atypically for the late 1970s, from his soul, not from chemicals. He was, as well, very tenacious.

As was the case, and as remains the case, that in most groups of young adults, lots of individuals have magnificent dreams. Jeff, however, was among the minority within our circle in that he persistently worked hard to reach his goals (at a time when many among us coasted on smarts). Furthermore, his focus was on working as diligently as possible towards achieving a goal, not on complaining.

I recall when he landed his recurring role with the (now defunct) *Pittsburgher Magazine*. Such an honor was rare among the college crowd, even among a group of young ones prepped by families and by faculty to become "achievers." His attitude toward his opportunity was rarer still. Jeff was not boastful, just busy. His professional accomplishment did nothing, in his mind, to separate him from the guys and gals with whom he was sharing his college years. His "big chance" was a personal stepping stone to which he meant to adhere, nothing more. Humility, too, was among his character traits.

In short succession, most of us graduated. Some of us took on additional education. Some of us did not (given that we were, mostly a bunch of engineers and computer scientists, the greater portion of our gang didn't have to bother with secondary or tertiary degrees to get desirable jobs). In addition, many of us got married, a large percent of which, as evidenced by the union of Computer Cowboy and myself, to each other. Babies came into the picture as did mortgages and others of the trappings of midlife.

Over the years, my husband and I moved away, first geographically, and then spiritually, from that coterie. We lost contact with many of our former friends. Intermittently, though, Jeff and I corresponded. I become an academic. He became an advice columnist, and a well-respected reporter, one who wrote for a major outlet. We still had words in common. We also still shared a history.

Tens of years passed. Jeff and I continued our informal communication. Meanwhile, my family took on the Torah way of life. Concurrently, Jeff received new book contracts. In one of his emails, Jeff shared his ability to embrace the entire spectrum of Judaism; one of his brothers was Orthodox, and, as such, was no more or less a brother to him than his more secular sister. There was and would be no judgment forthcoming from Jeff on my husband's and my journey.

After moving to the Holy Land and coming to the realization that I could not teach university-level rhetoric, since I lacked a powerful command of Hebrew (I was struggling with my *ulpan*'s, my school for the intensive study of Hebrew's, Level One), I returned to an old aptitude, creative writing. The Jeff who had cheered me on when a musical was produced that I had written during our undergraduate days, was the Jeff, who cheered me on when an older me received my first nonacademic book contract. He was not too busy or too important to give an old friend encouragement. In fact, his words are among the blurbs on that book's back cover.

Over recent years, I'm not sure whether his select, personalized missives, or his many general examples of modeling gracious professionalism were more important to me. Both forms of support were extremely valuable. In fact, a few months ago, when I received an email from Jeff, which apologized for the richness of his publishing two books in one calendar year, I saved that letter. I meant for his words to be a template for me; I was experiencing, in a good eye, similar good fortune. Sadly, that note also served, foremost, as the last message I have from Jeff. I've yet to delete that well-shaped piece of modesty.

Jeff's works, deservedly, found places on *The New York Times Best Sellers List* again and again. Not only was he an amazing human being, but he was also a very skilled writer. My voice is not needed to laud his work; both the big house publishers, which gave him contracts, and the highly visible folk, about whom he wrote, trusted him, based on his merit, to deliver superlative texts.

Like many individuals whose lives he touched, I, too, counted on Jeff to deliver unique human standards. I remember when he asked me why someone we both knew, who had made it big in the media, had refused an interview. Not wanting to utter derogatory speech, I said I wasn't sure. To Jeff, it was inconceivable that people could be mean-spirited.

Hence, I am at a loss. The Holy One, Blessed be He, took this very special individual, Jeff Zaswlow, when Jeff was only fifty-three, from this work. May Jeff have merit in heaven. Although his shloashim, the thirty days after his burial, has already passed, I have been unable to write, before now, about his transfer to The World to Come.

Jeff Zaslow was an extraordinary, selfless, and talented man. While his books, articles, and advice columns will continue to be celebrated for their combination of insight and sensitivity, it was Jeff's quality of loving kindnesses toward others that is his greatest legacy.

In *Pirkei Avot, Ethics of the Fathers*, we are instructed to be wise by learning from everyone we encounter. Accordingly, we would merit to learn from the unassuming Jew who was Jeff Zaslow, and from his character trait of loving all of the rest of us, no exceptions whatsoever.

Friends

I noticed she had wrapped her head not in her customary wig, but in a scarf, and I said as much as our two cars sped past each other, in opposite directions, on one of Jerusalem's main streets. In turn, she giggled into her dashboard phone; it had been too long since we had embraced. That afternoon, as well, a face-to-face meeting was not ours to be had. At least, we had had the opportunity to smile and to wave. Even that modest portion of shared experience meant a lot to us; we regard our friendship as precious.

Friends might be but a single component of a good heart (a good neighbor, and a good eye, i.e., judging other folks favorably, being the other ingredients), yet friends remain an invaluable life commodity. Moshe Bogomilsky reminds in "Questions and Answers on Chapter One of *Pirkei Avot*," that Rabbi Yehoshua ben Perachyah, the former leader of the Sanhedrin, said, "get yourself a friend."[11] Many commentators go so far as to translate Rabbi Yehoshua ben Perachyah's charge "get" as meaning, not just "acquire," but, also, if necessary, "pay for" making a friend.

Levi ben Gershon, The RalBag, i.e., Gersonides, explained in *Ha Deyos v'ha, Character Traits, The (Torah) Knowledge and the Personal Qualities,* that "paying for" a friend can include having to: tolerate their foibles, spend money on them, use up time or energy on them, and, maybe, for their own well-being, fight with them. That is, being a friend can mean having to shell out resources.[12]

But that sort of payment is not a bad thing; as Rabbi Pinchas Avruch, referring to the writing of Rabbi Eliyahu Dessler's *Michtav Me'Eliyahu, Letter from Elijah,* and to *Path Eretz Zuta,*[13] the portion of the Talmud concerned with "how we are to treat one another and with what traits of character we are to try to develop," states, in "Investment Strategy," that we love that into which we have to invest ourselves.[14]

In truth, I do not feel as though I forfeit, per se, for the sake of that gal pal of mine, the one who was driving toward one end of town while I was driving away from the same. I feel the obverse. She recites *Psalms* more meticulously than I do, and, when our families get together, she is calmer with, sweeter to, and generally more hospitable toward our joint crowd than I could ever be. Rather than fault her for those favorable qualities, I work to continue to be jealous of them.

I suffer in our relationship only in that I find it challenging to create ways to use my resources for her. She gives and gives and gives. I stumble to give anything to her. At least, when we lived in the same community, I could bring her, when I visited, Sabbath flowers or wine. These days, when many kilometers separate our domiciles, all I can provide for her, most often, is a listening ear.

Plus, concerning those respectful disagreements that color many friendships, they don't seem to season our talks. Rarely, and then only concerning topics like raising teens and twenties, or topics like ways to improve our attitudes about our absorption process, is discipline shared between us. Nonetheless, those always lovingly framed, sometimes uncomfortably stark suggestions that we make to each other are part of the value of our union.

A friend is a relation to whom we turn for aid in our personal growth. Rabbi Dovid Rosenfeld writes in "Peer Pressure" that "a friend is a true soul mate, one who influences us on the profoundest level." Rabbi Rosenfeld then reinforces his position by also citing Rabbi Yehoshua ben Perachyah;

> One who wants to succeed in life must acquire for himself a good friend.... With the support of proper friendships, we are capable of seeing far more in ourselves, delving far deeper into our souls, and defining and becoming aware of our inner selves. A rabbi or teacher can lecture to you for hours on end, but only when you and a friend together discover what life is all about will you truly discover G-d.
>
> Conversely ... nothing can be more detrimental than a bad friend [,] one who is unworthy and exerts a negative influence on you. Friends touch each other in the most intimate manner possible with their soul-bond and heart-to-heart discussions. Be touched by one who teaches you to live for yourself and ignore the beckonings of your soul—or one who sees friendship as a means of sharing gossip and bitterness—or one who betrays your trust and friendship, repaying you instead with manipulation and verbal abuse—and you will be hurt as deeply and intensely as the good friend can build you up.[15]

In other words, that cherished other of mine, that friend who had business at the opposite part of town, is precious to me not only because of the good influence she has on my life, but also because of the lack of bad impact she has on me. When I smile in her presence, it is not just because she is nurturing, but also because I trust her effect on me to continue to be beneficent.

True friends help us walk the path. They give us encouragement when we are down, and (strong) ethical guidance when we are being stupid. As psychologist and family therapist Emuna Braverman posits in "Friendship and Empathy," it is those people who help us feel joyous about our heights and, by implication, regretful about our lows.[16]

Accordingly, it was of no surprise than when I knew I would be heading toward the vicinity from which my friend was exiting, no matter how brief would be our anticipated encounter, I was excited to "see" her. We love our friends both because they nurture us and prune us and because we "pay for" them.

Inspiration from Ourselves

First, be a Person of Integrity and Honor:
Derech Eretz Kadma l'Torah

Wittingly or not, we live according to our personal schemata for merit. Some folks claim that their relationship to The Name is the highest order of good. Others espouse that their relationship to the rest of humanity needs to be their chief concern. We need to side with the latter, ironically *because* we yearn to please The Boss. The way in which we live our lives must precede our "religiosity."

Yet, the truth of the principle of *derech eretz kadma l'Torah*, of being a person of integrity and honor before all else, can't be actualized exclusive of Torah. Without the foundation provided by our strictures, we can't be certain of the nature of our "goodness" or of the most meaningful way for us to act, accordingly.

Fortunately, proper living requires neither hair covering, nor a commitment to learn in a religious program (albeit both of those items are useful and can help us evolve spiritually), but requires the taking up of the cause of "unity," as opposed to "uniformity." Our behaviors need not embrace all of everyone else's choices. Rather, Jewish virtue mandates that we remove ourselves from the unfortunate attitude of "them" and "us," or, more so, of "you" and "me." We need to try to feel affection for all Jews, and to try to understand that Jews have always been and will always be "us" and "us." In short, each and every person is precious, each and every person deserves honor, and each and every life is sacred.

We have to work at realizing these absolutes. In spite of the personal and collective legitimization of modern, secular mores, most of us still, as is appropriate, struggle to bring to light an attitude that dispenses with granting ourselves the right to judge the relative merit of others. We know deeply, as well as intellectually, that we have been commanded to cherish their and our own (often unknown) worth.

This Torah concept is not impossibly archaic so much as it is a challenge to our ordinarily complacent selves. On the one hand, it's easy to dismiss the importance of other people. On the other hand, it is vital that we celebrate their presence in this world by treating them first and foremost with every imaginable kindness. All of the above notwithstanding, finding an intact snowball on a desert would be far easier.

The fact remains, however, that it is more than sinister to regard other human beings as having, at best, relative value. Additionally, it continues to be more noble to grapple with our less desirable tendencies and to repeatedly fall, i.e., to repeatedly have to reboot our efforts, holding tight to The Almighty each time we slip, than to disdain even a single other human being. Consider that each of us is fashioned from the same combination of earthly dust and heavenly soul as are all of our brothers and sisters.

The sooner that we accept the necessity of prizing each other, the sooner that we will know lasting peace. If, alternatively, G-d forbid, we insist on failing to find the good in all people, all of the time, we make that most sought-after end difficult to achieve. The writing on the wall, per se, did not completely fade, relative to the mysterious script interpreted by Daniel in the time of Belshazzar. Rather, only the semantics have changed. These days, humans still irrationality evoke supernal graffiti, that is, we still draw divine attention to our imperfections.

Correspondingly, we suffer sickness, financial insecurity, familial woes and many other problems. Egocentrically-focused reality causes our governments, too, to trip up. Perhaps, most gravely, such a tack, the presumption that we are vindicated in adjudicating other persons' worth rather than in doing our utmost to improve our side of relationships, is a form of idolatry, of fallaciously trying to raise ourselves above our designated station. Grimly, in acting in that way, we choose the curse, not the blessing.

While it is easy to attempt to explain the soundness of reacting negatively to persons more strict than ourselves, who, for instance, might give us discipline about the type of buttons we have on our shirts, or about persons less strict than ourselves, who, for instance, might invite us to concede their view that we ought to abandon the mitzvah of keeping the laws of touching, it is neither wise nor correct to yield our closeness to each other over our differences. Just as drivers traveling faster than us are not, in truth, "maniacs," and just as drivers traveling slower than us are not, in truth, "demented," all other Jews, living at their points of the observance array are not better or worse trekkers. Together, we're on the only available highway.

Last time I checked, I was Jewish. Such an appellation does not mean that I am from a particular part of the world, that I hark back to an extended family that lived in a certain way or another, that I cover my hair with one type of modest wrapper rather than with something else, or that I eschew prayer cantillations that are unfamiliar to me. Rather, the reference "Jew" marks me as: awestruck by The Almighty, needing to constantly work on my character traits, and revering the Holy Land and the Holy People.

Accordingly, given that my husband and my kids hold similar views, our friends tend to range across the entire array of Judaism, in a good eye. In recent weeks, bless G-d, we attended weddings, Bar Mitzvah festivities, circumcision gatherings, and engagement parties celebrating Chassidic, Modern Orthodox, Sephardi, and Litvische families. My family is blessed.

Regarding my family's Chassidic friends, although my knees no longer allow me to take part, I love watching the festive dancing that these friends facilitate at weddings. Joy is essential to serving The Holy One, Blessed be He, as well as is a telltale sign of faith. When we Jews act sincerely on the belief that The Boss is driving the bus, we have no reason not to be happy.

As per my family's Modern Orthodox pals, it's important to exclaim the success with which those dear ones integrate select parsimonies of the greater world with complex Torah values. For instance, at a Bar Mitzvah feast, the parents of a celebrant born during the Torah portion of Noach, made sure that the hall's surfaces were decked with comestible abundance as well as with collections of plastic critters. Whereas the youngest guests were enamored with the many available bowls of candies, the pancake station, and the cake table, those children also made sure to claim fistfuls of lions, tigers, and bears. We slightly more mature partakers were impressed with how our friends had used an often trivialized Torah portion, and had transformed it into something both palpable and memorable.

Later that week, some of my family's Sephardi friends, as is their wont, set new standards for Jewish hospitality at an engagement party. Words of Torah flowed. Guests were greeted at and later ushered past their door.

Many introductions were made among well-wishers. There was a place for all visitors. Many smiles were shared. I lingered, not wanting to leave.

As per our Litvische friends, all comers to their party found themselves among true princes of Israel, given the Torah speeches we heard. At that celebration of a Bar Mitzvah boy, the apparel of the host and his family was elegant, the food was served unobtrusively, and cute, yet practical, gifts were given to all participants. However, the most important aspect of our friends' warmth was the care that they gave to the very young, to the very old, and to travelers that had journeyed literally across the world to attend the festivity. Royalty, among Jews, as evidenced at that happy occasion, remains not just the province of lineage, but also of manner.

In a settlers' community, outside of Jerusalem, my husband and I again sat among Jews gathered together for a wonderful reason. At that yeshuv, we welcomed a future scholar-warrior to the tribe. After the bris itself, we sipped, supped, and talked of ways to advertise the glory of our Maker. Among the scarf-covered heads and knit yarmulkes, the depth of our covenant with The Almighty was clear. Loyal Jews cleave to the imperative to use all of our internal and external resources to attend to the ways of Torah.

During the next few weeks, with the help of heaven, Computer Cowboy and I will join with other families, who are special to us, at additional festivities. May it be the case that such exultations continue to show the Nation of Israel's devotion to The Boss! May it be the case, as well, that such communal excitement continues to join together Jews!

Blessings are necessary to life cycle events. Torah speeches are integral to them. Food, drink, dancing, and other forms of shared delight are either required or are traditional at such junctures. Nonetheless, it is our collective observation of these vital moments that helps keep us front and center, which enables us to honor The Name. Our festivities remind us that our heterogeneous Jewish communities truly are concentric.

Unity

Wow! Having spent the first forty years of my life following a stream of Judaism that is not the same as the one my nuclear family embraces today, and having always welcomed all flavors of Jews to my home, to my table, and, otherwise, to my life, it does not fail to surprise me when any Jew attacks me, privately or publically, in print or by spoken discourse, directly or implicitly, for being "different" from him or her. I don't understand, and hope I never will grasp, the need actualized by some of us to categorize members of the worldwide Jewish community.

Whereas I might elect to purchase food with select kashrut certification for my home, or to encourage my oldest child, who is in the marrying portion of life, to date certain sorts of young man, I neither deride other Jews for their kashrut choices, nor insist that my daughter necessarily limits herself to certain boys (So far, for example, her suitors have ranged from hilltop settlers to black-hatted fellows. I pray only that the right young man, i.e., her future spouse, will make himself known at the right time). My friends, and my extended family, for that matter, range from "nonobservant" to folks of the long *payos*, sidelocks, persuasion.

A Jew is a Jew. *None* of us have been given the authority to decry the worth of another member of The Nation of Israel. *None* of us ought to waste a single, precious moment of life doing so.

Consider that the entire array of us was counted when the silver half pieces were collected thousands of years ago. Consider that the twelve tribes are related branches, not separate entities. Consider that even if we fail, G-d forbid, to regard ourselves as united, our enemies, as evidenced by *The Shoah*, The Holocaust, and as evidenced by contemporary politics, consider us a single people.

So what gives? Do any of us really have the spiritual luxury to spend our resources, or really have the moral shamelessness to cause other Jews to use up their resources, on base behavior, that is, on broadcasting prejudice against each other? I doubt it.

Let's reboot. Let's try to focus on what we share. Let's stop weighing whether or not someone has a yarmulke on his head, and, if so, what the nature of that covering is. Let's stop looking at whether or not someone has a beard, and, if so, what type. The "face" we present to ourselves, and less importantly, to the world, needs to be one of alliance.

Not only are we at risk of delaying the rebuilding of the Temple because of our inexcusable hatred, and at risk of delaying the coming of *Moshiach*, the messiah, because of our unjustifiable disgust with each other, but we are also at risk of losing the land that is dear to us, G-d forbid, and, more personally, of losing ourselves. I disbelieve that those are the outcomes we seek.

In contrast, when we cleave to each other, miracles happen. The Name smiles on his children's efforts to get along together and rewards us with good ends.

So, I say to the religious "leader," who attacked me in print, because I said that I love The Brotherhood of Israel far more than I love our enemies, and I exclaim to the guest, who ridiculed me for deigning to have sufficient mind and mouth to object to being sidelined because I did not dress exactly like some other women, get over yourselves. If you have rhetorical prowess, please do not use it to fuel the designs of the evil eye, to further splinter our people.

Rather, please use your gift of words to help us act decently toward each other. Your contribution towards our people's unity counts as much as does mine, and maybe, your interest in our common well-being, which The Name yearns to hear, counts even more.

Pepper and Salt

My friends and I joke that I wear my glasses on test days because they make me smart. I might look smarter, but unfortunately, my specs have no affect on my abilities. The only reason I wore them to the *bagrut*, matriculation exams, I had today was because one of my eyes was hurting from my contact lens.

First impressions are the strongest, and it's peoples' exteriors that we look at first. So, basically, how you look is how people think about you, often forever.

For example, when I wear my glasses, I look "smart." When I don't wear them, I look "blonde." I've learned to wear them when I have an interview because they give me a look beyond that of "the-blonde-next-door." Without them, I am boxed into the "blonde" category, or into the "female" category, or into the "Israeli" one. Some things I just can't change.

It doesn't matter if my glasses are the shape of Harry Potter's or the thickness of the pile of my overdue chemistry lab reports; they don't change my brains. Amazingly, the same is true about other things, too. Big things, like disabilities and like learning differences, changeable things, like piercings and hair color (the closest I have ever gotten to dying my hair was permanent marker. Don't try it, especially if you are blonde), and unchangeable things, like skin color, don't alter the insides of a person.

Yet, people judge each other by those things all of the time. People judge before they know the person whom they are judging; that's called pre-judging, as in pre-judice. It's not right.

A child in a wheelchair is no less able to read than a child who can walk unaided. Someone who dresses in black and has a hole in their eyebrow doesn't necessarily present more of a threat to society than does the math teacher who lives down the block and wears a tweed suit. Blondes are no more air-headed than are people with other hair colors. We just have bad publicity.

A study was conducted where two dolls, identical except for skin color, were placed in front of children. Each child was then asked to pick out the "nicer" doll. A wide range of children were tested. The majority chose the Caucasian doll. Even the dark-skinned children chose the light doll. Why? They had learned prejudices.

When we judge people for how they look, and not for who they are, we not only hurt the ones we judge, and ourselves, we also hurt those who learn from us. Being big means having responsibility. Being big means thinking before you act... and thinking before you judge.

A blonde walked into a bar. Ouch.

— Rivka

"Black and white," "chocolate and vanilla," "pepper and salt," and many other, similar phrases have been and currently are employed in reference to gradations in skin tone. Such rhetoric, however, is racial. What's more, interestingly enough, race is not a biological, but rather, is a social construct.

Much as we have chosen to separate ourselves into strata based on secular education, on car make, on residential address, or on other such superficial nonsense, it seems that we have also elected to allow ourselves to be divided by flesh tones. Certainly, we don't protest when such behavior occurs. We could take a lesson from dumpster cats who appreciate that "race" is a frail means of ascribing rank.

When the welfare of those cats' young, the maintenance of their habitat, or the availability of their rations are endangered, they fight turf wars. Yet, those beasts never battle about who has stripes or who is marked with splotches.

In their limited ability to appreciate their corner of creation, those animals never regard taupe as superior to ochre or gray as better than beige. Though they position themselves according to might, rather than according to justice, they are not duped by strictures based on historic power plays (check your college text books if you doubt this claim about the origins of racial prejudice). Their community standards are based on welfare.

What's more, consider, in North America, the nuance of skin hue has long dictated social standing. Buses, housing districts, and water fountains were relegated according to melanin. In Europe, too, for hundreds of years, chromatophores were scapegoated as the rationale for the persecution of entire communities. Ironically, the eye or hair color that made an individual an elite in one country were grounds for enslavement in another.

Throughout the world, including, sadly, in the modern State of Israel, differences in pigment, as that variable expresses itself in outward appearance, not only impacts criteria for beauty, but also impacts criteria for schooling and for employment. As is true elsewhere, these prejudices are based on regional values.

For instance, three of my children, though direct biological offspring of dark haired parents, lived their first years as natural blonds. Two became darker in skin and hair as they aged, but one retained most of her Russian looks. That child, more than her brothers and sister, has been, since immigration to Israel, the recipient of all sorts of chauvinism, ranging from drivers harassing her, to classmates accusing her of dipping into peroxide, to teachers treating her as ditzy.

In this Old World, her sister, a girl who developed from a fair-haired toddler into a young woman with olive skin and darker locks, is considered normal. Since many of our friends and neighbors immigrated from Mediterranean or Middle Eastern regions, light complexions, here, are considered "odd" or "artificial."

Until we recognize, and then dismiss, entirely, the utility of using color as a social place holder, we will continue to be accountable for allowing others' politics to determine the eventualities of our lives. Such ends are wasteful. In the least, Israel, the cradle of civility, ought to be colorblind. Phrases such as "black and white" ought to be relegated to cookies, and "terms of endearment," which refer to pigmentation, ought to be cast from our common language.

— Hannah

Just Smiling and Nodding

It's great to be blonde. I have a built-in excuse for any stupid thing that I do. My new favorite "stupid" pastime is petting the stray cats in The Rova, The Jewish Quarter of Jerusalem's Old City. Those cats are tame and friendly, and they offer a good break from my National Service. When people see me petting cats, they look at me and smile and nod, thinking that I'm "blonde." The truth is that my "stupidity" has no connection to my hair color, as seen by the fact that many brunettes are "stupid," too. When I catch someone of a different hair color acting "dimwitted," all I can do is smile and nod.

For instance, a few weeks ago, when I was petting a purring and nuzzling cat, while seated on a bench in The Rova, a pair of tourists sat down next to me. About a minute after the tourists sat down, someone I knew came over. I turned to talk to her. The cat, which was offended that I had stopped petting it (since I'm "blonde," I can do only one thing at a time) jumped off of my lap and started to smell the tourists and their pizza. By the time I turned back to the cat, it was eating the tourists' pizza and they were cleaning it with a baby wipe.

"She's covered in dust," the tourist explained to me. I smiled and nodded.

After finishing the pizza, the cat jumped back onto my lap. The tourist offered me the baby wipe to finish cleaning the cat. I didn't explain to her that the cat would only get dirty again, or that cats know how to clean themselves. I merely smiled at her, again, and told her "no thanks."

The "smile and nod" is a great defense mechanism, unless those individuals against whom it is employed catch on. A smile and nod differs greatly from a "grin and bear it." The latter is what you do when you have no choice about a matter; you have to do it. That's the "bear it" part. The "grin" is that you might as well do it happily.

"Smile and nod" is different. That gesture contains a special nod which actually means "no." When you smile and nod at someone, you are actually saying that you think they are "stupid." There is nothing affirmative about that nod; rather, it shows you are amused.

By the way, "smile and nod" can be used at home, too. My mom asked me to clean my room this morning. I smiled, nodded, and turned to the next page of my book.

— Rivka

To me, "smiling and nodding" is the art of containing one's strong feelings in the face of blindness to social norms, in the face of ineptitude, or in the face of downright meanness. This behavior is one way in which folks can stay detached when confronted with provocations. It is an inappropriate means of dealing with abusive or with otherwise toxic interactions, but it's suitable for mundane stupidity.

Although some articulated irritations hurt worse than do ant bites or than do first degree burns, such annoyances are often best left alone, i.e., devoid of further stimuli. Consider, as a case in point, the woman, with whom I yet remain pals, who said, "Hannah, you've lost weight. You must have been beautiful once." Alternatively, regard the child, for whom I dragged myself out of bed extra early, after a late night of problem solving with that kid's sibling, who announced, "But I don't want your blessings for the new school year. You're such a nerd. You don't understand teenagers."

My husband fails to grasp why I tolerate such verbal arrows. While he's not of the opinion that I ought to return or even to deflect such shows of aggression, he does believe that I ought not to have to endure such chin wagging. Unfortunately, short of avoiding all of my friends and family, I am unable to comply with his wishes.

Rather, I assess my dear ones' nasty words for what they are, rhetorical debris that gets mixed up in interpersonal communication. I can no more prevent those close associates from dropping rhetorical crumbs on me, intentionally or otherwise, than I can keep visitors from tracking all manner of dirt into my home. In either case, my best strategy remains determining whether and when it's worth cleaning up what's left behind, and then leaving matters alone.

This morning, for instance, one of my cherished people asked to borrow my cell phone since that individual forgot theirs at a friend's house. Likewise, minutes earlier, I received a call from a hair dresser who was
98

cancelling my daughters and my long-awaited haircut appointments because a more lucrative deal, specifically, eight women who wanted hairdos for a wedding, had come through. In the former case, I mildly replied, "No, you may not." In the latter case, I scheduled time for us with another stylist. In both cases, I just smiled and nodded.

— Hannah

The Merits of Counting

It's *Safirat HaOmer*, the time of counting. We are counting from the time of our exodus, of our physical redemption, to the time of our immigration to Israel, the time of our spiritual redemption. In the case of the former, we are returned mastery over our bodies. In the case of the latter, we are given mastery over our souls.

Every year, we make this trip. Every year, we have the opportunity to appreciate its wonder. Every year, we can experience this period of counting as a gradual progression to the height, which is Torah, and as a literally step-by-step means to rebuilding ourselves.

Even so, Shavuot, the celebration of our greatest gift from G-d, Torah, is not the only apex toward which we move higher. Even so, the iconic sheaves of grain, the *omer*, are not the only significance we count. Mere mortals, both our *Tikkun Olam*, our reparation of this world, and our reparation of ourselves, necessarily have to be completed piecemeal. Both are finite sets of procedures that cannot be poofed to conclusion, but must be actualized via our methodically working as diligently as possible towards achieving them.

It is relatively easy to talk about ending political corruption, to muse over making our media truly free, to espouse principles for flattening the fiduciary tiers of our health care system, to chant about championing the environment, and so forth. In spite of that communicative downrightness, it remains far more difficult to actualize those models than to neglect to do so. Utopian dreams are dandy for tableside discussion, but, in "real time," such talk accomplishes little more than strain on our organizations. In short, there's lots that is wrong with a worldview that rejects objectivity and that embraces a prescriptive set of ethics.

For instance, the idealistic upstart who checks colleagues for paperclip pilferage might be refocusing corporate resources at the cost of missing egregious sources of pollution, at the cost of overlooking his or her company's standing history of gender-based harassment, or at the cost of failing to notice "straightforward" money laundering or identity theft problems.

Likewise, the "do-gooders," who petition against strategic settlements, or who use their public recognition to elsewise undermine Israel's sovereignty, might mean well, but indubitably act foolishly. It takes sagacity, patience, tenacity, and, above all, faith, including, especially, the willingness to listen to The Name's instructions, to partner with The Boss in repairing society. Bandying about one's ego is less than a poor substitute for obedience and devotion.

Similarly, personal growth is a somewhat nonlinear, always gradual process, which depends, ultimately, on The Almighty's aid. Even prophecy, at some point, is no more than the collecting and the reassembling of fallen heavenly pieces. So, it makes sense that we count: the days until we can use the mikva, the three weeks of tragedy, the months of *Shmittah*, the agricultural Sabbath, and the years until a boy's first haircut.

More mundanely, but no less miraculously, and for the same reasons, we count: the months of gestation, the hours a baby sleeps at night, the number of teeth establishing themselves in a toddler's mouth, and the rate at which preschoolers "get into trouble." Later in life, we count the days until a child's wedding canopy, a grandbaby's first steps, and the number of visits our generations extend to us.

Whereas many of us purchase, for ourselves or for our loved ones, tallitot, which have tzitzis already tied on, and whereas many of us buy bakery-made challot, it remains our responsibility to count the number and kind of knots in all of those fringes. Likewise, we're accountable for sending them to a storage area in a synagogue or in a cemetery that is designated for worn out books and papers, on religious topics, if they are beyond repair, and it continues on as our obligation to make sure that we buy our Sabbath and holiday bread from sources that have "taken challah." Counting is inseparable from Jewish living.

Correspondingly, though we might hire babysitters to occasionally mind our sons and daughters, and though, when they are older, we might employ matchmakers to help them find their help-opposites, we parents remain accountable for their development. Both our sacred and our secular lives are built from the fixed rhythms of our efforts, as guided and enhanced by G-d; they are not built from any instantaneous magicking of results.

Furthermore, there is a cosmic type of counting in which we engage. Whereas we cannot count on the world to love Jews, we can count on The

Name not to abandon us, His people. Just as we are experiencing an increase in overt anti-Semitism, we are concurrently experiencing an increase in immigration to the Holy Land and in increase in individuals' service to the worldwide Jewish community.

Sure, some of us persist in claiming that the way in which we build ourselves and the way in which we build our culture is neither subjective nor open for interpretation, i.e., that we, as individuals and as a collective, possess the ability to determine our destinies. Yet we never have, never will, and currently do not live in an alternative, cognitively-driven reality like that of *The Matrix*. Romantic notions and other misinformation aside, we live beyond such a pretend world, in a reality where we can attain even higher levels of living than we can imagine with our limited minds. Such is the nature of finite beings counting toward the infinite.

Moreso, such is the nature of The Holy One, Blessed be His compassion for us. As Rabbi Lazer Brody writes in "Counting the Omer," "true freedom, which includes the liberty from social pressure and bodily urges, comes only from Torah. Therefore, even though we break off the chains of bondage at Passover, we're not really free until we receive the Torah 50 days later on Shavuot."[17]

During the confluence of events that we call the seven weeks of counting, specifically, and during the tallies within our lifetimes that each of us merits to go through, more generally, we are elevated to reach for luminous bits, to impact the quality of our individual comings and goings, and, on occasion, to prove ourselves more broadly useful than we had been earlier. How can we be anything but grateful for the opportunity to tot up our bits and chunks? How can we do anything save for making happy music, sponsoring children's processions, participating in parades of the trees' first fruits, giving over joyful words of Torah, or dedicating all-nighters to Torah learning, once we realize the benefit of calculating our individual and communal ascensions?

Counting might be tedious. Counting might be boring, but reckoning with the seemingly insignificant portions that build us up is both import and rewarding. During our lifetime, may we be blessed to find meaning in the adding up all of our own and our loved ones' steps!

Wardrobe Unsavvy

My mom and I have different ideas about dress, to say the least. In her opinion, black is the new pink. It's also the new blue, the new green, and the new everything else. In fact, it seems to me that black is all she ever wears. Luckily, I gave up on my mom's outfitting long ago, around the same time that I started to worry about my own.

As I was the first grandchild, and a girl at that, I never had a shortage of clothing. My baby albums hold proof of the crazy clothes I wore. The experience might have been a 90's thing, but I'm leaning more towards a "what a cute baby, lets pretend she's a doll" thing. While I don't remember any of it clearly, I can picture myself lying on the bed and looking at whoever was dressing me at the time with an expression that must have said, "why are you stuffing me into this itchy outfit that I'm going to spit up on in twenty minutes, anyway?"

I can't say that my attitude towards clothes has changed much. Sure, I stumbled upon *fashion sense* the same time that I got acne and noticed boys, but I was never into makeup, pink, or heels. I don't know that I ever will be.

Unfortunately, my lack of enthusiasm for the latest fad isn't good enough for my mom. While my style is more "boyish" then "girlish," I still unarguably have the body of a girl. Even though I don't wear tight shirts, I do prefer short skirts, and shorts underneath them, something that my mom is against.

Thus, each morning I need not only wrestle with the monsters growing in my (all right, I'll admit, *messy*) closet (they think it's a sock swamp or some other prime fiend hangout), but with my mother as well.

"Bye mom," I yell to her, grabbing an apple for lunch and running out the door.

"Come back here, what ARE you wearing?"

"Ummm...." I look down at myself. I'm wearing a shirt that I "borrowed" from my brother; I liked the color, a short jean skirt and no shoes. Darn, where are my shoes?

"The shirt isn't tight." Defensive is best, no?

"And the skirt?"

"My school doesn't care, as long as I promise to keep my shoes on." One too many barefoot run-ins with the school secretaries have given me a new dress code.

"And what IS that sticking out of the bottom?"

"Leggings?" Is this a trick question?

"What's the rule about leggings in our house?"

"Last year you let me!"

"If I see leggings sticking out one more time...." I decide that it's simpler and less time consuming to roll up the leggings then to try to explain why I need them. On second thought, maybe not.

"Why do you even wear leggings?" my mom continues.

"To jump over fences." The truth is always best, right? "Normally, I wear shorts, but they are all in the wash."

Luckily for me, my dad honks the car horn then, signaling just how late I am making everyone else.

"See ya, Mom!" I say, grabbing my sandals on the way out. Another sweet victory.

— Rivka

Queen-sized, middle-aged women, such as myself, have often been accused of many unsavory things, in part, because we are earthy, steadfast, and opinionated, and in part because we often dress in frumpy ways. When we ladies are also mothers of teenage daughters, we are likely to be subjected to lots of comments about our wardrobes.

My teenage daughters, for instance, think "frumpy" ought to have been left behind in my grandmother's Lower East Side neighborhood or in her grandmother's city of Vilna. In my girls' esteem, lack of stylishness has no business in the lives of contemporary, Middle Eastern, Jewish women.

It is not so much that they eschew my dangling earrings or my multiple head scarves. If arranged according to my girls' tastes and in hues that suit them, such accessories of mine are "acceptable." Moreso, it is the case that they question my sneaker-plus-jumper look and have articulated disdain for my layering of shirts. In short, my teens do not want it to be broadcast that theirs is a dowdy-looking mother.

Albeit, I have publicly admitted that I am challenged by knee socks that seek my ankles and that I am more interested in attending to my poetry and prose than I am in attending to my attire. However, I contend that if my clothing is clean, modest, and seasonal, I look anything but shabby.

In fact, I am beginning to believe that my daughters' protests are a means of diverting my attention away from their clothing choices. Perhaps our family's youngsters, not me, our family's matron, lack stylishness.

To wit, I bring to your attention my daughters' penchant for layering skirts, for wearing dozens of bracelets, and for garbing themselves with impossible combinations of shirt-like garments. Whereas the girls cover up all of their bits, their fashion sense leaves me wondering whether or not they have given sufficient thought to finding the most aesthetically pleasing means to cover their bodies.

Granted, popular color combinations in this Old World run according to Old World, not according to New World, prescriptions, and granted, my little ladies, alas, have fully bloomed into teenagers with all of the concomitant attitudes of that developmental stage. Yet, I sometimes find it difficult to understand why they match certain tops with certain bottoms.

To date, the teens and I have declared an uneasy truce. They make only half as many faces at my clothing choices as they did just a few months ago. I, likewise, am better than I was just a few months ago at limiting my comments on their selections to remarks about whether or not their outfits are modest.

Nonetheless, there remains a tension among our closets. The kids wish Mom was more up-to-the-minute. Mom wishes the kids were more traditional.

Consequently, we are an unmatched, at times passively hostile, set of family members, who remain convinced that the other parties could not possibly know what they are doing when it comes to making choices about apparel. The good news is the kids will grow out of it.

— Hannah

So Much Clap Trap

When I was a small, secular, American girl, being "Jewish" meant wearing a silver-plated Magen David, donating regularly to the JNF, The Jewish National Fund, and driving to synagogue for Sabbath. I understood my winter holiday not as an acknowledgment of my forefathers' sacrifices, on behalf of keeping our people unassimilated, but as a "Jewish version" of my school friends' celebration. I liked to help my classmates drape tinsel on their trees, too, since I adored pretty things.

My Rosh Hashanah and Yom Kippur were days when my synagogue was more crowded than usual and when services were longer than usual. The only other remarkable quality of those occasions, to that earlier version of me, was the plating of honey cake for New Years and of bagels for breaking the fast after The Day of Atonement.

Those many decades ago, I went to secular dance halls, wore the most contemporary of clothing and makeup, and had no qualms about debating alongside of boys during interscholastic high school forensic tournaments. At that time, too, I looked forward, when my family made interstate trips, to eating Howard Johnson's most popular dish of the 1960s (hint: that foodstuff is not indigenous to landlocked cities).

Yet, I identified as a "Jew," was the "Jewish Heritage" chairperson of my tristate counsel's youth group, and proudly wrote for a newspaper whose audience was my region's Jews. More exactly, I served, first as a teen columnist, then as an intern, and later as a college columnist, for Pittsburgh's *The Jewish Chronicle*.

While associated with that paper, my myths about Jewish life slowly shattered. For instance, although I had long held food that did not conform to Jewish dietary laws of kashrut to be wonderful, my chief editor refused to promote non-kosher food in my writings or to allow me to further any such an idea in his pluralistic newspaper. In spite of that, I had been "so far removed by the Gypsies," that I didn't even know what kosher food was or whether or not anyone actually still ate it. I had never seen men who regularly wore yarmulkes, women who covered their hair, or children who realized that the aleph bet was a means to a significant end rather than an end to itself.

Although that kindly senior journalist was among my first guides, my path to greater comprehension was anything but linear. Consider that during my college years, one of my greatest indignities was not that a holy structure, my university's sukkah, had been vandalized when swastikas were spray painted on it, but that my right to protest such doings was questioned.

I was attacked, repeatedly, in my university's student newspaper, by another Jew, for writing about the incident. That antagonist and I volleyed back and forth until our university's dean of students declared both that there would be no further publicized debate on the topic and that a committee would be formed, by the administration, to investigate matters of religious violence.

It's great that the dean was a defender of civil rights. It's a pity that Yours Truly failed to comprehend that the social desecration of a place of sanctity was a far bigger issue than was my relative freedom of speech.

In balance, at the time, although I was determined to date only Jewish boys, having figured out that I was getting old enough to get married, I had no problem eating, drinking, and making merry with friends of all types. "Jewish," to me, was a suit of attitudes I put on for certain occasions, or a posture I assumed in response to certain situations, not a way of life or a perspective integral to my very being.

Not until my junior year, as a liberal arts major, did it occur to me that my heritage might be distinct from the presentation of "Judaism" offered up by my country of origin's melting pot. Accordingly, instead of waiting until the winter, when my campus would be enlivened by that other holiday, I insisted that all of the Jewish people I knew join me in a party room, which I had reserved in my dorm's basement; we would celebrate the High Holidays by eating honey cake. I had much to learn.

In graduate school, during days free of classes, I worked at the only Jewish place of worship in my university's Midwest town. I became further appalled. My students' parents blamed me, a young teacher who met with their kids for only two hours per week, for any gaps in their children's basic knowledge of our heritage.

In my muddled mind, I considered that, perhaps, parents ought to relay important life teachings, to serve as the link from the generation before them to the generation after them. I mused that parents ought to transmit Judaism to their children. Something was beginning to click; my dissonance with my contemporary life was increasing.

By the time that my husband and I got married, we asked an Orthodox (!) rabbi to officiate. We were yet so distant from observance, however, that when the rabbi said he was bringing a Sabbath observant witness to our union, we had to ask him what "Sabbath observant" meant.

We had sought that Orthodox rabbi not because we had suddenly become enlightened, but because I was desperate for a counterweight to the deprecating rhetoric that my husband and I had received, during a premarital counseling session, from a leader of another stream of Judaism. That leader had focused on all of the ways in which a partnership could go wrong and on all of the ways in which people hid, rather than rectified, "bad" behaviors.

There had been no talk, from that man, of the sanctity of marriage, of the responsibilities of man and wife toward each other, of the Jewish People's weddedness to The Name, or of anything remotely positive or sensible. I was unwilling to start life with only his sorts of "blessings."

Despite the fact that we were fortunate to be married under Orthodox auspices, my husband's being called up to the Torah, as a groom, on the Sabbath before our wedding, proceeded without him, and I had no bridal preparation. We were hitherto ignorant of the cornucopia of goodness which was our birthright.

Decades passed. We didn't hear The Name when The Name whispered, so He Shouted. Finally, not one, but a series of life and death situations caused my husband and I to question the epistemology upon which we were basing our important decisions. We were fortunate that our foundation was shaken while we were still young; we were only forty when we became observant.

Amazingly, we found ourselves heirs to a comprehensive blueprint for living. That revealed design has been successfully perpetuated, for thousands of years, the worldover. Torah Judaism, we discovered, provides a guidebook for how to eat, how to dress, how to sleep, how to parent, and much, much more.

In short time, my family's perspective shifted. Academic awards lost their sheen relative to mitzvot. Success, as measured by salary, took a backseat to domestic harmony.

More time lapsed. The Holy One, Blessed be He, didn't require us to give up all comforts; He required us *to be willing* to give them up. For example, although I never applied for a second set of funding from the National Endowment for the Humanities, I did receive multiple Pushcart Prize nominations. Similarly, although my husband tailored his work life to suit Sabbath and holiday observance, he got promoted anyway, in a good eye.

Our kids became math whizzes or able artists notwithstanding the fact that their school days were longer than had been ours. Further, our kids, in a good eye, experienced ordinary adolescent *angst*. Nevertheless, unlike their mother and father, they received, from our religious environment, social and spiritual support, which enabled them to pass through those obstacles relatively cleanly. Plus, our sons and daughters regard the major holidays as a time of reflection and renewal, hope and happiness. If they have honey cake alongside their prayers, it is a bonus, not a focus.

Rhetorical Altruism

Last year, I read an account of a New World home infested horribly with snakes; it was filled with of hundreds of them. The more that the home's owners tore their walls apart, the more snakes that they found. "Bad" became "worse." The family filed for bankruptcy. Their bank foreclosed on their house.

Interestingly, the locals had long regarded that building as plague-ridden. Yet, those others had said nothing to their new neighbors when those unfortunate folks were considering purchasing that house and said nothing to them, thereafter.

Lashon Hora, a derogatory speech about another person, exposure to which is a similar predicament of being overrun by pests. It is hidden, and, when uncovered, it most often proves extensive. As well, many people, who are aware of this problem in themselves, or in others, say nothing about its existence or about its worsening state.

Not surprisingly, the result of our collective disregard of this trouble, like the result of our collective, occasional exposing of it to the light, does nothing to prevent our going into spiritual bankruptcy. Likewise, our communal lack of response to this infestation of the soul creates a situation in which The Great Bank eventually forecloses on us.

****

Consider the goings-on in the weekly Torah portion, "Shelach," in which ten of our twelve spies speak against the Holy Land and against following The Name's command, and the goings-on in the weekly Torah portion *Korach*, in which a book smart, but otherwise dim, person chooses to stand with the evil eye, to situate himself beyond the rules and to bring down, literally, a significant portion of our people.

In the former case, not only did we rebel against The Land of Israel by saying Egypt was the land of milk and honey, but we also rebelled against Moses, our teacher, The Holy One's chosen representative. In the latter case,

110

not only did we nay-say the established social order, but we joined in a growing insurgence without giving heed to the reasoning behind it or to the near future consequences of our actions. Korach's sons did not descend very far and they "reemerged" from Purgatory to this world sometime later, because they were mutinous, but also mindful.

We are taught, accordingly, that The Name forgives our sins against Him more easily than He forgives our sins against other Jews. We have the red heifer to redeem us from the *eggel hazahav*, the golden calf, and we have the slow reflourishing of the physical property of the modern State of Israel to amend our ill-regard of the same.

Yet, when it comes to bad will among humans, to an absence of *bein adam l'chaveiro*, to an absence of proper personal behavior, such absolution comes less readily. It's bad to speak against The Name. It's worse to speak against The Name's creations. The Boss has infinite understanding and knows that he does. We lack such a great quantity of kindness and benevolence. Subsequently, The Boss holds us more accountable for hurting each other than for spiting him.

****

Listening to or following calumny, or listening to or following true but disparaging remarks, too, in the least hurts us, and at worst, kills us. Evidence the punishments mentioned above, which we suffered when acting thus. Rav. Saul Wagschal reminds in *A Guide to Derech Eretz,* i.e., *The Path to Living Ethically and Responsibly,* that "a human being is held responsible for the damages he cause[s], even inadvertently."[18]

We know, instinctively and cognitively, that foul speech about Jews, about The Name, and about Eretz Israel is wrong and that such rhetoric whether created, enjoined, participated in (even passively), or used to focus on our real or perceived faults is a nest of quickly multiplying snakes, the likes of which ought not to be ignored, minimized, or kept hidden.

The greater heat that surrounds us is not the prolonged hot weather of the region, in which temperatures approaching and passing 100 degrees Fahrenheit, and months without precipitation, are the norm, but the incalescence rising from within us. Too often, we toss about fiery words without regard for the harms such flaming might cause to ourselves or to others.

Even during this inauspicious period of *Bein ha-Metzarim*, of Between the Straits, i.e., of The Three Weeks, a time of mourning over the destruction of the Holy Temple and over our exile, when certain activities are forbidden since we are supposed to decrease joy and inspire mourning, and during the historically further ill-fated span of the Nine Days, when additional activities are forbidden, we continue nonetheless to heedlessly kindle interpersonal fights and to fuel many ill-advised fancies. In brief, we seethe, we sear, we scorch, and we scold with our mouths. We ignite without heed of boundaries or of consequences.

****

Such persistent engagement in derogatory speech about another person might derive from our: not bothering with mindfulness, feeling insecure, placing other people's opinions of us above The Almighty demands on us, or our making too little of an effort, too late, to morph problematic character traits into good ones. Yet, understanding, i.e., minimizing, denying, or rationalizing, "causes" for our behavior hardly excuses it. Melting, roasting, incinerating or otherwise turning others', as well as our own souls to ash, continues to be inexcusable.

To begin with, it's insufficient to claim that we want our actions to be a tribute to The Name. The opposite holds true, too. We sincerely assert that we don't want to hurt other people, but five minutes after making such statements, we have no remorse when pointing to the lad who dresses differently from his parents, to the girl who committed to one type of *Sherut Leumi,* or army service, instead of to another, or to the elder who davens a little faster or a little slower than we do. Derogatory speech about another person is about truths, not about fabrications. We create problems by citing veracities, not by spinning fictions.

Additionally, we do not always strive to be altruistic. Too often, it seems, we attack other folks to mask our insecurities. This poor social prestidigitation buries us, our subjects, and our listeners. Whereas we could use Torah "as a crown for glory [, instead we use it as] a shovel with which to dig."[19] Just as Korach got into awful trouble for his imagined grandeur, so, too, do we when we insist, directly or implicitly, that we be regarded with high repute and that, concurrently, our neighbors, teachers, students, parents, children, friends, colleagues, and the like, be regarded with lesser esteem.

What's more, we allow ourselves to be entangled in the threads of what we believe others think about us instead of fearing The Name. When confronted with this truth, we disown it or whine. Consider, in illustration, the following mashal from the collected writings of the Chofetz Chaim, *Give Us Life*, *Moesholim* and *Masterwords of the Chofetz Chaim*;

> *Several domesticated critters ran in through the gate surrounding a family's home and garden. Before being herded away, the goats, among all of the animals, ate up many of the family's greens. The family vowed to each other to keep their gate shut in order to prevent further damage.[20]*

Nonetheless, as time passed, the family forgot its vow to guard the entrance to all that they held precious. Pigs ran in, dug up the roots of the surviving plants in the family's garden and gobbled them down.

The members of the family no longer trusted each other to keep their vital portal closed. The father walled off their lone entrance.

Thereafter, to enter and leave their homestead, the family had to climb over the wall. The mother and children complained that such effort was both arduous and degrading. Not unkindly, the father answered that it was better to suffer from difficulty and humiliation than to die of starvation.

Similarly, it is better for us to lose social standing and to experience hardships that to be denuded of all of the goodness we glean in this world. In the World to Come, there will be no such opportunities to nourish our souls, no new gardens of opportunities to improve our inner selves.

****

Finally, we posit that we ought not to bother guarding our mouths because it's too late and we're too far gone for any chance at bettering our spiritual well-being. Interestingly, not only have we no right to judge ourselves so harshly, but it is also the case that it remains essential for us to make amends, especially in this most important area of our lives.

Another mashal, also by Chofetz Chaim, also from his book *Give us Life* explains;

> *A bricklayer customarily took his lunch break at a beach near his worksite. One day, while walking on the sand, he discovered*

that a myriad pearls had washed up. Yet, he did not bother to collect those precious bits, justifying his behavior with the semi-plausible account that since he had only half of an hour left of discretionary time with which to scoop of some of that treasure, his take, relative to the whole, would be paltry.[21]

Even with "half of a lunch hour" left, we need to make the most of the assets available to us. We need to go back over our actions and to correct, while we are of this world, any that seem less than commendable. Our way with words, first and foremost, needs to be amended.

Our inability to keep our moths shut is the worst of human-fashioned ovens. Purgatory is nothing relative to the way in which we currently are killing ourselves. Our not-too-covert mention that a dear one's kashrut might be one off, that a superior probably cheated on taxes, that a cousin drives too close to other cars or drives too far away from them, and those grumbles we articulate, "just between us guys (or us girls)," about this municipal clerk or about that doctor, create a worse condition for us than does any other form of human degradation or cosmic comeuppance.

We need to not keep roasting in this infamy. We need to not heat up additional communication complacency. Solutions to our problem of derogatory speech about another person are not: beyond us, explicable, less worthy of our attention than social status, or insurmountable.

It's hot outside. However, it's sweltering within. Recall that when we engage in derogatory speech about another person, we harm ourselves. We need to return to a better place regarding this behavior of ours. Fortunately, there exist accessible means for us to improve this character trait. These means include: not participating in derogatory speech about another person, not believing any derogatory speech about another person that we might unfortunately read or hear, and engaging, regularly, in Torah talk.

Per the strategy of not participating in derogatory speech about another person, beyond not uttering or writing such ill-fated sentiments, when exposed to others' utterances of the same, we can: change the subject, stuff our ears, or walk away from such talk. First, refraining from referring poorly to other folks solves a lot of problems. Second, when we are exposed to such lapses in judgment, we can change the subject (albeit, we have to be careful not to embarrass a speaker, since that act, itself, is ethically problematic). Third, we can wedge our lobes into our ears so as not to actually, physically, hear any of the low thoughts being expressed. Finally, we can pick ourselves up and walk away.

114

Per the first item, there is fleeting social recognition for persons who bring "juicy" information to conversations. In balance, though, there are long lasting, cosmic consequences for behaving in that way. Essentially, it's better to shut up than to be taken to task later.

Per the second item, individuals who like burnished "news" about associates are often the sort who can be distracted, fairly easily, by other shiny things. There's merit in refocusing a rotting piece of dialogue toward some frivolous, immaterial topic. Additionally, it's fairly easy, in general, to redirect the attention of superficial thinkers.

Sometimes, though, folks are so invested in just how superior they feel when expressing or witnessing derogatory speech about another person that it's difficult to draw them away from such bad topics. Such occasions are times when it's advisable to employ physical barriers to listening.

A snood, wig, hat, set of ear muffs, or other accessory, pulled tightly down over the sides of one's head or shimmying up to an overworking heater or air conditioner can, sometimes, help block out the sound of bad words. Other times, one can surreptitiously (again, it's important not to embarrass other folks, i.e., not to substitute one bad choice, listening to gossip, with another, public humiliation) stuff one's fingers, ear lobes, or what-have-you into one's ear canals. It remains far better to seem "one off" to peers than to be judged, by Heaven, as having fallen from the righteous path.

Sometimes, none of the above works. In those cases, one must not slide toward noisy appliances, but entirely walk away. It is better to become unpopular for leaving an Earthly conversation than to be "unpopular" for eternity.

Another repair, beyond distancing one's self from derogatory speech about another person, is disbelieving derogatory speech about another person. Even if, G-d forbid, one has already heard derogatory speech about another person, it is possible not to believe it.

We can assume, when we hear poor reports of another person: that there could be some justification for a person's alleged "wrongful" actions, that the person rendering the telling could be mistaken in explaining what he or she saw, that the person rendering the telling could have left out some crucial parts of the tale, and that the story, as a whole, could be exaggerated. While it takes a little effort to try to reframe information according to these suggestions, energy employed thusly is more than worthwhile in that the consequences of such an expenditure can result in our being free of the *averah*, of staying from the path, of derogatory speech about another person, and can result in our being positioned to urge others to rethink nasty reports.

Finally, beyond not participating in derogatory speech about another person and beyond not believing any derogatory speech, which we did not escape, we can more positively impact human communications by adding more good to the world. Specifically, we can engage in Torah talk. Whereas each and every ill-advised set of words must be amended and cannot be compensated for, it is also the case that acts, which bring light, help to dispel darkness, including the darkness of derogatory speech about another person.

In *Nefesh Hachaim: Rav Chaim of Volozhin's Classic Exploration of the Fundamentals of Jewish Belief*, Rav Chaim Volozhin points out that "If two people sit together and there are no words of Torah between them [theirs] is a session of scoffers."[22] In other words, one way to stay fallen down is to fail to stand up. Torah talk can't "balance" our bad choices, but it can create an atmosphere in which such choices are less likely to bloom and in which the problems created by such choices are more likely to be addressed.

Torah talk can elevate our interactions, in general. Such words can help us move away from the habit of derogatory speech about another person, in particular.

Avoiding derogatory speech about another person, disbelieving derogatory speech about another person, and creating a communication environment in which derogatory speech about another person is unlikely to thrive, all are means that are accessible to us for combating this horrible human tendency to speak poorly of other people. As a people infused with integrity and honor, it behooves us to employ these tools to better our lives.

A Little Perspective

About a year ago, I was watching some kids on Sabbath. These kids came from a Charadei house in the Charadei part of our neighborhood. It was my first time taking them out since my sister, who normally watches them, was sick. It was a kindness she performed so that their mother could attend a learning session for women.

I took those kids to the park to play on the slide, encouraging them to climb the ladder. I fed them wafers when they came down. Everything was going well. The kids had warmed up to me, a complete stranger, and the day wasn't too hot.

With a smile, I sat down on the side of the park to rest. I overhear a mother talking to her daughter. "You see that girl over there," the lady asked. Her pointing finger and stare made it obvious.

"Yes, Mommy," the girl answered.

"We are not like her. We don't act like her. Don't learn from her."

To say that I was shocked would be putting it lightly. At first, I had no idea what the mother was talking about. What was wrong with taking children out to the park? Sure, they weren't my kids, and sure, I had never met them before, but they seemed to like me, and I had always believed it was good to be helpful.

Confused, I looked back at the mom and followed her glare. The problem was my skirt.

In place of the simple a-line skirt and opaque stockings that graced her and her daughter, I was wearing a wrap-around skirt and sandals. As a result, I was considered to be a "horrible person."

That unfortunate mother presumed to judge my character based on how I dressed. She chose to overlook my actions and to concentrate on my seams and on my lack of socks.

I believe that dress is a reflection of the inner person, but I also believe that we should look past dress.

That uncomfortable afternoon, I was dressed in accordance to "The Law," i.e., per her interpretation of it. Although I wasn't wearing stockings, I had not suddenly become a bad person.

Sadly, not everyone is able to get past appearances. People judge others all of the time. People judge level of religiosity, intelligence, integrity, and wholesomeness, based on clothing.

In my esteem, though, one who wears jean pants and not a jean skirt is no worse a person than one who wears a strimmel and a long overcoat. It's not the clothes that make the person; *it's the person that makes the person*.

I left the park sad that day. I wasn't hurt by the comment; I knew that it came out of naivety. I was sad because that lady's daughter would grow up learning prejudice.

— Rivka

At various times of my life, I have been blameworthy for stereotyping according to material artifacts. Said more plainly, I've been guilty of assuming that folks who are more stringent than me about certain things are necessarily morally superior, and that folks who are less careful than me are necessarily morally inferior. I've come to discover that such beliefs are based on fluff and nonsense!

Simply, whereas there might be a correlation between the length of one's skirt, the nature of one's head covering, and the number of buttons fastened on one's shirt to one's relationship to G-d and to man, there also might not be. Integral goodness is the potential province of all persons. What's more, most of us have lived through experiences in which the behavior of folks, whose lives seem radically different from our own, and whose actions we had assumed we understood, surprised us.

I've been treated with unabashed integrity by persons wearing half as much clothing as me and by unabashed disdain by persons wearing equivalent amounts. I've seen individuals who are "tight" with The Boss push their way into lines to buy premiere sports tickets, to get "good" parking at cultural events, and to snag the optimal among available vacation rentals. I've also witnessed persons, who have no visible connection with The Holy One, Blessed Be He, run: to hold doors open for the elderly, to rescue stray animals, and to put handfuls of coins into beggars' cans.

The opposite has been true, too. Folks not-yet-Sabbath-observant have had no problem speeding through neighborhoods, on Saturday mornings, windows down and speakers blaring. Some of those persons don't mind elbowing their way through outdoor markets or parking in manners that endanger other drivers.

In short, I'm fatigued by the constant rant I hear about "those other guys." *We* are "those other guys," no matter the level of our spirituality, the way in which we cover our bodies, or the manner in which we formally educate our children. Each of us is responsible to treat each other with integrity no matter our opinion of what the "proper" lifestyle ought to be.

Imagine a community in which the residents treated each other with boundless dignity and in which neighbors failed to take it upon themselves to judge and to punish individuals who acted differently than did they. Imagine peace within our tribe.

It behooves us to remember that each of us is valuable and that each of us was created because each of us is needed to heal our community, to make us whole. It behooves us to act a lot more kindly as well as a lot more considerate to our fellow Jews.

— Hannah

Controlling Attribution of Meaning

One does not need a terminal degree in behavioral science to come to the common sense understanding that we prejudice our interpretation of events by the words that we use. Consider, for instance, two terms (and their semantic relatives), seemingly polar in meaning; "Charadei" and "punk." Read the following exposition twice, using only one of those terms, or those terms' relatives, in each of your readings. If you do not have two very different effective responses (feelings) to the two resulting, vastly different versions of the same narrative, you are not being honest.

For instance, the sentence "I live in a religious/rough neighborhood" should be read as "I live in a religious neighborhood" or as "I live in a rough neighborhood." The sentence "Other women/punkers entered the bus" should be read as "other women entered the bus," or as "other punkers entered the bus."

Please keep in mind that in developing this exposé, I am not trying to slur either type of lifestyle (it is not for any of us to judge each other, merely to build fences around the behaviors we value); I intend only to point out how labels (mental or articulated) can impact, strongly, on how we feel about a group of people, regardless of their character attributes. I hope that this exercise is a bit incitant in the sense that I hope that this exercise provokes mindfulness about how we treat each other.

Meanwhile, I don't understand. I guess I have not yet fully acclimated to this culture. Under these conditions, I am not sure that I fully want to acclimate.

I live in a religious/rough neighborhood. I like where I live. Some of the sections are more to the right/conventional. Some are more to the left/more counterculture. It is possible, by living here, to be friends with and to learn from an array of people.

There is variation in my neighborhood. Some women wear snoods/nose piercings, some wear sheitels/eyebrow piercings, some women wear scarves/tongue piercings, and some wear hats/tattoos. Some ride the regular buses. Some ride only the mehadrin buses/buses on which punkers and members of the establishment are segregated.

Depending, mostly on my mood, I wear: a snood/bejewel my nose with a piercing, a sheitel/bejewel my eyebrow with a piercing, a scarf/bejewel my tongue with a piercing, or a hat/reveal my tattoo. I happily ride either the regular bus or the mehadrin bus/bus on which punkers and members of the establishment are segregated.

In the morning, I love participating in the "book club on wheels;" I love sitting among other women who are davening *Psalms*/punkers who are reading the lyrics to anti-establishment music. In the afternoon, I am often juggling just to figure out where to put my backpack, my packages, and my feet.

In the morning, if I ride a segregated bus, the "women's section"/"punkers' section" is often partially filled by men/old members of the establishment. That's fair enough; few Bait Yaakov girls/energetics ride at the hour that I travel, yet many men/old members of the establishment are making their way to yeshivot/their daily groove. In the afternoon, the opposite is true; many Bait Yaakov girls/energetics are coming home from school and few men/old members of the establishment are not yet returning from yeshivot/their daily groove.

Given the above axioms, I am utterly confused about what I experienced on the bus today. The women's/punkers' section was very crowded. There were, literally, about a handful of men/old members of the establishment in the front. An enterprising woman/punker sat down at the back of "the men's section"/"the old members of the establishment's section" and beckoned for me to follow. So far, no problem.

Two couples, each which seemed composed of a wife and a husband/of an old member of the establishment and of his punker friend, too, took seats at the back of "the men's section"/ "old members of the establishment's section." Also, so far, no problem.

Many, many seats remained empty at the middle of the men's/old members of the establishment's section. In an area ordinarily filled by four people, one man/one old member of the establishment sat. Also, across from him, in an area ordinarily filled by three people, only one man/one old member of the establishment sat. There were other empty seats.

More and more women/punkers got on the bus. Men/old members of the establishment left the bus, but for a while, no men/old members of the establishment got on.

I invited the man/old member of the establishment, who was sitting in front of me, to move from the area for three to the area for four, where the other singular man/old member of the establishment sat; such a move would vacate an area meant for three people for women/punkers.

He ignored me. My Hebrew is not that bad.

Later, as pregnant women/punkers got on the bus (and refused to take my offered seat; I guess I look older than I feel), I again invited the man/old member of the establishment to move to where other men/old members of the establishment sat. I also asked a learned-looking man/compassionate-looking old member of the establishment, who had since seated himself with the lone man/old member of the establishment sitting in the four person area, whether that learned-looking man/compassionate-looking old member of the establishment might also invite the man/old member of the establishment, in the three person area, to move to the four person area.

Perhaps, I ought not to speak to men/old members of the establishment to whom I am not related. That behavior, itself, is legitimately frowned on in many circles. As a woman/punker I possess a different social clout than do men/old members of the establishment.

Exasperated, the man/old member of the establishment, who was sitting in front of me in the three person area, turned around and said to me, in a clear voice "No! This is a mehadrin bus/a bus on which punkers and members of the establishment are segregated." Ever so indignant, that man/old member of the establishment glared at me and at the other women/punkers near him, while avoiding even acknowledging the presence of the pregnant women/punkers holding onto the straps above his seat. Thereafter, the man/old member of the establishment opened up his cell phone.

When that man/old member of the establishment left the bus, the pregnant women/punkers took his space for three since his departure left that space completely empty. Other women/punkers entered the bus.

My difficulty is with the inconsistency. Whereas I have no issue with separate seating for men/old members of the establishment and women/punkers, and whereas I appreciate all the good that derives from such behavior, I do have an issue with double standards.

Why is it okay during periods in which more men/old members of the establishment travel on buses for men/old members of the establishment to fill part of "the women's section"/"the punkers' section," but not okay, during periods in which more female riders/more punkers travel, for women/

122

punkers to slide up the partition of the men's/of the old members of the establishment's section? Even at places of prayer/concerts, mechitzot are shifted to accommodate the proportions of various demographics of a crowd.

I will continue to enjoy my religious/rough neighborhood. I will continue to enjoy community davening of *Psalms*/community reading of lyrics to anti-establishment music, per se. I will continue to enjoy segregated buses. I will, as well, continue to be mystified by some individuals' behavior.

And Then Came Kislev

Light. A completely dark room, so it's said, can be transformed by a single candle. Similarly, a seemingly hopeless situation can be altered by a small amount of faith.

This Kislev, like the Kislevs that preceded it, I witness all manner of anguish. In my family, in the families of people dear to me, and in the families of strangers, as brought to my attention by organizations that support The Nation of Israel, I behold great trouble or woe.

A woman suffers either from a brain tumor or from clotting in her parietal lobe. A man is jobless. A small child must endure either surgery or drugs that will leave her unable to go to school, to eat, and to sleep. A family goes bankrupt.

As well, a youth drops out of school, a young adult gives up on seeking an arranged marriage, again, again, and again, plus an elder, a cherished member of a community, dies. Additionally, a middle-aged man endures a crippling injury.

In the background, rockets fall from enemy lands, despite international pressures to cease and to desist, or to at least to pretend to do so. Children scream all the way down to their communities' bomb shelters.

Global heavyweights, meanwhile, dictate political strictures that make sense, perhaps, after quantities of absinthe, hookah use, or unrelenting insomnia. "Non-observer" status gets declared on a wild tribe without land, infrastructure, or local history.

Then my headset rings. A friend collects for cancer victims, works to fund more clinics here. Another mom raises money for children with diseases so horrible as to make military leaders cry. At our front door, a beggar asks for coins and then blesses the next in line, among our offspring, that he should marry soon.

Former colleagues remember me and each other across the Internet, through phone lines, and by snail mail. Someone's sister yields a favorite dessert for someone's brother. Eye glasses, orthopedic shoes, and also canes get donated to needy individuals.

Tomorrow remains as unknown as bone marrow. Today, clouds intersperse with sunshine. Humming birds visit my window box. Last year, I hosted mosquitoes.

I think about my buddy, the one who had had back surgery and who now jogs miles. I reflect on the once unloved little girl who currently revels in a husband and in three small children. I contemplate the immigrant who couldn't find employment in his former field, but who has, instead, built up a successful career in a new one.

Life is nothing like our plans, but almost always better than our expectations. Last Sabbath and this Sabbath are the darkest ones of the calendar. No matter—last week, I lit candles and ushered in the Sabbath Queen.

This week, too, I will light candles and usher in the Sabbath Queen. What's more, after Sabbath, I will kindle my menorah.

Keeping House during a Sudden Illness

When I was little, I had a purple playroom. The room was that color when my parents bought the house. For a while, it kept its plum carpet, its lilac curtains, and its mauve walls.

My mom hated those colors and wanted to repaint it. I loved my playroom. I don't know that I ever registered the "creativity" of the color scheme, but I know that I loved the neverending possibilities that the room offered.

In one corner, I took care of my myriads of dolls (courtesy of the "she's-the-first-baby-and-a-girl-at-that" syndrome). There was also the corner with the "fire-station," i.e., a few boxes painted red, where my younger brother was chief, and the drawing table area where my younger sister would busy herself becoming the next Degas or Van Gogh. Sometimes, we three made a museum of all of our toys. Other times, we had an eggplant-colored castle, from which parent-type dragons came to eat us.

On one occasion, our playroom became a supermarket. I pretended that I was a rich mother. My babysitter played checkout girl. I came to her with a purse (Mom's castoff) full of construction paper money. I was well prepared to purchase my basketful of plastic foods. Our till was an overturned plastic tub. Our bags were borrowed from beneath the sink in the kitchen. My "heels" were years too big, but that didn't matter to me; what mattered was that I was like Mommy. I was doing the things that she did.

Now, over ten years later, I am once again doing what my mom does. This time, however, the doing involves shekels, not construction paper, and frozen meat, not fake fruit. This time it's real, not make-believe. My mom is sick and I'm making Sabbath.

It's not that I don't know how to cook. I'm actually pretty good, judging by the amount of food, cooked by me, that gets eaten. It's not even that I'm cooking much more than I normally do; I'm taking shortcuts by buying fish sticks and cake. It's just that Mom isn't here to tell me what to do.

Making the shopping list and handing out chores, in real life, feels like my playroom shopping trip from years ago. The experience is an adventure, but the shoes don't fit right. I'm not quite ready to take this walk.

It's easy for me to complain about the way things are done when Mom's well, and that I would do it so much better if I were in charge. But when it really comes to my being in charge, my "new ideas" are the ones Mom implemented years ago. In fact, those ideas are the very things that keep our house running. While it's a good experience for me to make Sabbath every now and then, I think I'll leave the job, as a whole, to Mom, at least until my feet grow some more.

— Rivka

We do not plan for disease or damage. These experiences, nonetheless, enter sometimes into our lives.

Without being graphic, I will share with you that my health has spun out, once more. My family has canceled guests for months of Sabbath dates, for our Purim festive meal, and for our Passover ritual service and ceremonial dinner.

Computer Cowboy, when he's in the country, attends teacher meetings, drives to the grocery store, and addresses the larger issues of running our home. When he's out of the country, those things slide.

Meanwhile, our gang of teens, whom I'm proud to call "sons" and "daughters," strive for normalcy. Their "regular" tasks, such as tidying their rooms, running the garbage to the dumpster, sweeping, helping with laundry, and helping with dishes, remain in place. In addition, there are new responsibilities for them to complete.

Someone has to go the corner store when Dad's not home. Someone has to censor visitors and phone calls until Mom is well enough to devote energy to such matters. Someone has to supervise the younger children. Someone has to make tea.

Someone, sometimes, too, has to take on the tasks, which Mom would ordinarily actualize, and which cannot be ignored. Sabbath preparation, during the early weeks of my illness, was one such matter.

The first Sabbath that I was ill, I couldn't get beyond my bed clothes and the bathroom. I didn't care what was prepared, how it was prepared, or who prepared it. I didn't even care about residual messes. I'm glad my husband was in a land far away; he would have been saddened by the conditions here.

The second Sabbath that I was ill, I was able to change into Sabbath apparel, but didn't have the energy to prepare more than one meal's worth of soup. I was unable to sit up for any entire meal throughout the twenty-five hours, and chose instead to continue my communication with my family from a nearby sofa. At least, Computer Cowboy was back in town.

The third Sabbath, I sat a bit longer at the table. Going to synagogue was not even close to being a dream. I appreciated, instead, having to take only two naps.

Before the fourth Sabbath, my doctor permitted me one ten minute outing to an outdoor market. I slept almost four hours after that "adventure." At least, I was able to be the source of my family's favorite hummus and of fresh fish.

Before the fifth Sabbath, I made a fifteen minute outing to an outdoor market. I slept that afternoon and all of the next morning. Thereafter, I made both soups and one of the main courses for our Sabbath meals, in a good eye, since I was feeling a little better.

Preparations for the sixth Sabbath found me completing most of my culinary responsibilities (the teens ordinarily prepare salads). Bless The Name, I was able to stay at the table for most of each meal.

By the seventh Sabbath, I was able, in a good eye, to stay at the table, fully, for each meal. I even engaged the children in word play, thereafter.

This week, nearly two months after my diagnosis, I hope, with the help of Heaven, to walk to synagogue. My doc said I could try it.

Sudden illness makes us appreciate the mundanities that we take for granted. I'm looking forward to climbing the long staircases of my hillside neighborhood. I'm looking forward to taking back all of my duties from my children.

— Hannah

Looking Backward: Looking Forward

At this juncture, during which time I am unwillingly being caused to consider that my kids are getting older, I try as much as possible to cheer them on from the sidelines. Awkwardly, I work to accept that my offspring's' tribulations belong to them, and not to me and, subsequently, that their failures or victories are theirs, as well. More specifically, as long as their growth opportunities are neither dangerous nor destructive, my job is not to interfere, but to remain in the bleachers as an observer.

Sure, alternative means of adjudicating the ebbs and flows of the lives of sons and daughters exist. Some moms insist that all of the emotional dingers, which are experienced by their children, ought to be brought to those moms, and that when their kids are in their teens or twenties, that only they can "protect" those "innocents." Other moms champion the notion that after certain, seemingly arbitrary spans, that they, the moms, ought to have nothing but short, polite interaction with their kids.

In my esteem, both of those responses are unwarranted. Per the first reaction to kids' growing up, I believe it is vital to understand that unpracticed children make for underdeveloped adults. That is, it's in our children's interest for us to limit ourselves to elevating their good deeds from afar and to limit the wibbles and wobbles about which we are wont to exclaim. Ringing up the relatives about each accomplished goal of our children is of small worth, as is honking to any available audience about all of the bad choices made by our offspring. Moms can't and ought not to closely referee their older kids' lives.

Not all difficulties, which press against our offspring's growth, are evil. Making mistakes makes for sound experience. Regression, including temporary backsliding, *is* compatible with development. My offspring's shortcomings are no less important than are their spurts of progress. However, the former are increasingly less and less my business and the latter are decreasingly, at least in the physical milieu, in evidence.

Per the second above mentioned reaction to kids' growing up, why bother being a parent if that role means divesting from children when they get too big to carry? Older children need moms' input more, not less, as they grow into adulthood. Just because we can't lift them away from intrapersonal or interpersonal conflicts, as we could when they were toddlers, doesn't mean that our boys and girls no longer need us to show them how to separate themselves from strife. Moms can't and ought not to abandon their kids during their kids' later stages of development.

Not all alleged achievements are sunny. Comprehending the finite nature of success makes for maturity. "Attitude," including temporary grandiosity, *is* compatible with development. My offspring's incidents of overreaching are no less important than are their occasions of regret. However, the former are increasingly less and less my business and the latter are decreasingly, at least in the emotional milieu, in evidence.

My children creep out from my heart toward the greater world and then return to me, each time fledging a little farther than the time before. Such arrangements for their accessing their futures draws their strengths out in ways that no amount of my literally sitting on the sofa and crying, metaphorically wringing my hands, or figuratively pulling away from them, toward the horizon, ever could. They need me to witness, but not to herd, their development.

Children of mine, who stumble, Bless G-d, know how to pick themselves up, dust themselves off, and look backward, toward me, even when such retrospection is governed only by sentiment or kindred forces. Mostly, they look ahead; it's tough to walk on a balance beam when you're looking over your shoulder all of the time. Those kids grasp that Mom has not cast them off as much as she has loosened her hold.

While I watch from afar, I try to remain grateful that I am learning new parenting skills and that I an doing so willingly. Whether or not I'll ever garner the sort of parenting proficiency truly needed for a mom with kids who have advanced to their current respective stages of life, or not, is moot. I am the only mom my sons and daughters will ever have and I can only perform at a level that is a wee bit higher than my best efforts.

Sure, I might be better served, temporarily, by telling tales, by diverting my attention to others people's comparatively younger offspring, or by closing my ears to "the music." However, I live in this world, a world of action. The World to Come is the world of comfort. Children are rewarding. Raising them is not necessarily relaxing.

What's more, my choices, no matter the phase of any of my children's development, remain instrumental to their growth. In the very least, I model, wittingly or not, how to parent kids at each particular stage. At best, I am somewhat successful. Somewhere, somehow, subconsciously, my children will recall how I nurtured them when they were in their teens and twenties, when they were in high school, when they were in college, when they were in army, and when they got married.

Supposing that the future is the "elephant in our living rooms," with which we might avoid interacting, when it farts, it's hard to ignore its presence. Parenting older children is entirely unlike parenting younger ones. Most of us moms both value and dread this portion, despite the facts: that we knew our kids were going to grow up, that we prayed for their health and longevity, and that we worked toward those ends.

The span of life that brings us children who are emerging adults is an awkward portion. It's okay for us to uncomfortably enjoy it.

Inspiration from Joy

A Limited Time Offer

Dating is like drinking fresh milk; the newer the issue, the more likely the "health benefits." That is, it's unfair to stall decision-making when seeking matrimony.

In balance, "sell-by" dates are often posted way in advance of spoilage and many products retain freshness even after such deadlines. That is, it's important to *thoroughly* discern whether someone is the person who will complement them perfectly or not before concluding one way or the other. Mindful dating usually requires multiple sessions of sampling, of trying to figure out if someone is meant to be a life partner.

The list of questions that follow are prompts I've written for my *bnai bayit*, my daughters-of-the-heart, for kids I've tutored on seeking an arranged marriage, and for my oldest, who is currently in the dating "portion." Most of these questions pertain equally well to intendeds of either gender; some pertain only to boys. All are meant to help youth discern among potential mates.

* What is your relationship to G-d? What do you feel is His relationship to you? How do you currently serve The Name? What are your plans for service for the near and far future?

* How do you see yourself among Jews? Which demographics, e.g. race, ethnicity, worldview, make you uncomfortable? What do you with that discomfort?

* How do you currently aid the worldwide Jewish community? What are your plans for aiding the worldwide Jewish community in the near and far future?

* Have you explored the immigration to Israel process, i.e., do you know which steps are necessary for completing all of your paperwork? Do you know how long, at best, and at worst, each of these steps will take? For how long must you return to your country of origin to make this process happen? Does the Ministry of Education recognize degrees from the schools

where you learned? Do you have an arrangement for shipping over any desired belongings? Why did you elect to learn in Israel and why for that period of time? Discern among what you thought you should do, what your parents and other people thought you should do, and what you really wanted to do.

* Are you willing to make sacrifices to continue your studies? Temporal? Financial? Other? What is your level of dedication/commitment to Torah? What are your intentions for studying? How do you conceptualize your love of The Almighty? Love of Torah? Do you aspire to receive ordination? If you had to abruptly stop formal learning, what would you do? Half-time or full-time *kollel*, advanced study of the Talmud and rabbinic literature and work? Part of the day? Other? Did you and your parents discuss how you would support yourself/be supported if you married before finishing full-time learning? How would your rebbe feel if you left full-time learning? Now? In a year? In five years? In ten years? For how long would you, ideally, like to sit and learn?

* How will you deal with financial independence? (This question is especially important for young people unaccustomed to thinking about this issue.)

* Have you talked to the appropriate government offices about National Service obligations? Would you return to kollel? Learn and serve in a "hesder-style" program? Other? What type of service would you seek? Intelligence? Tanks? Desk job? Other? How do you feel about having a wife and kids while being in a dangerous situation? How would you provide for them while engaged in army duties? If something, G-d forbid, happened to you?

* How do your parents handle frustration? What do they do? How do you handle frustration? What do you do? What do you plan to do to develop stronger character traits in this area? What steps have you taken to change? What types of things frustrate you?

* How do your parents handle conflict? What do they do? How do you handle conflict? What do you do? What do you plan to do to develop stronger character traits in this area? What steps have you taken to improve in this area? How do you handle conflict with siblings? With friends? With parents? Between parents' and rabbis' wishes? How would you handle conflict between your parents and your spouse's wishes?

* How do your parents handle fear? What do they do? How do you handle fear? What do you do? What do you plan to do to develop stronger

character traits in this area? What steps have you taken to change? What frightens you?

* What would you do if you were angry? Sad? Angry with your spouse? Hurt by your spouse?

* What would you do if, G-d forbid, something tragic happened within your family? Within your spouse's family? To you? To your spouse? To your children?

* How many credits/hours/whatever do you have left to complete your degree? Are you planning on pursuing graduate work? How will you balance Torah study and professional life over the long run? What does your father do?

* What type of religious education did either of your parents have? What type of learning (study partners, lectures, other) do they currently pursue?

* Where do you see yourself in one year? Two years? Five years? Ten years?

* Why are you seeking a spouse (beyond peer or family pressure or sexual attraction)? Do you parents support the idea of you getting married, now? How old were your parents when they married?

* What does a functional marriage look like to you? On a spiritual level, what do you think the respective roles of a wife and of a husband are? On a practical level, what do you think the respective roles of a wife and of a husband are?

* How would you integrate children into a life full of learning: Torah, work, health, and building a marriage? Do you think that child-raising responsibilities ought to be divided? Who teaches the children Torah? Who guided your religious education? Who taught you pragmatics, e.g., the basics of getting along with people, cooking, going to the market, ironing, etc.

* Do you have a rabbi or other accredited teacher with whom you would be comfortable taking groom or bride classes?

Parenting a Daughter in an Arranged Marriage

Why should it surprise me that the daughter who went intrepidly to group babysitting at age one, because she felt so secure with her primary care provider—me, specifically, and with her world, more generally—went almost two decades later to college and into the dating "portion" without a need to check and recheck the truth of her home base? Why should it surprise me that this child stumbles, gets up, trips again, gets up again, and so on, almost fearlessly, in seeking her husband?

She was, as well, tenacious as an elementary school child, ever seeking to go hand over hand on the high parallel bars or to slide face first down on the chute. She had no fear of patting llamas several heads higher than her or of making friends with street cats, in a good eye.

Still, I tremble a little. Unlike fostering trust among the residents of the ark, mastering the playground equipment, or believing Mom will return for you when Mom's done swimming laps, finding the right partner necessarily includes thinking about things. Trust is not mastery. Seeking an arranged marriage requires being mindful about: attraction, religiosity, livelihood, matters of self, and over everything else, being mindful about character traits. What's more, while every series of dates does not end as a happy tale, with proper guidance, each series can increase one's level of self-responsibility and decrease one's level of unmitigated longing (and that's just regarding Mom... image the impact of such mindfulness on Daughter).

Fortunately, seeking an arranged marriage also involves The Name. When this daughter was being born, during a period covering two days and two nights, The Name helped her get to this reality. I believe The Name is likewise helping her get to her next stage. Her parents cannot proceed alone.

Granted, when my girl traveled to this world, I was brave at first, only wanting to give up on labor when Sabbath turned into *Motzi Shabbot*, the period immediately following Sabbath, and when *Motzi Shabbot* then turned into Sunday. Chaperoning the introduction of someone new was much harder than I had anticipated.

Sure, my husband, along with my midwife, encouraged me. Nonetheless, only I contracted and expanded, contracted and expanded, physically and cosmically.

A short time before my daughter crowned, during the part of labor that is the most difficult (as I came to learn, later, with her siblings), I decided to nap. As I fell asleep, I semiconsciously began to sing to her to urge her to join us. She answered and arrived.

I turned to my husband, before even passing my daughter's placenta. I told him that she was more than wonderful than anything I could have imagined and that we ought to begin, literally right away, to work toward having more children (natural labor is mind-altering, in the least).

Just as I had no idea how to bring a baby into the world, I have no idea how to help a daughter become a bride. Just as physical labor and delivery are intense experiences, so, too, are developmental labor and delivery. Both require focused attention. Both change the participants. Both sorts of births start quietly and privately long before being trumpeted as completed.

Sadly, the grandeur of both has been masked, in too many cases, by socially sanctioned "drugs," or by socially sanctioned "twilight sleep." Similar to the list of unnecessary birth interventions, the list of unnecessary matchmaking interventions is long and dire.

For example, many young adults suffer emotionally immoderate or otherwise zealous relatives, who "gift" young ones with large amounts of unsolicited advice instead of proceeding naturally. Such "do-gooders" fail to sit down with their charges and *to listen*, preferring, instead, the pill or potion that will render the seniors' transition least painful.

As for me, I am imperfect, strong-spirited, and, I hope, faithful. For this daughter, I intentionally labored and delivered at home, in my marriage bed. Likewise, I am intentionally chaperoning her through her current passage at home. The comfort of my sheets and towels has, decades later, become the comfort of our early morning talks and late night sighs. There is neither need nor reason to look outside.

Inside, we are good, strong, and safe. We are dancing as partners, no matter that the music changes. Yesterday was about embracing. Today, I release her and I release me.

When my daughter's father and I, as guided by advisors, determined she was ready to seek an arranged marriage, by dint of that change, we simultaneously determined that she was ready to start a home and a family. May The Name bless my child in her journey through this portion!

May The Name bless me, too! My husband claims he has never heard me cry so much, or so often, as I have cried during these transition weeks, except when I was pregnant with my girl (or with her siblings). I told him I am again getting ready for new life.

The wedding canopy is rebirth. We mothers feel its energetic intensity and we sense the early stages of labor.

Bride and Groom

Two weeks after immigrating to Israel, my husband and I merited, Bless G-d, to attend a wedding in the Old City. A bat bayit of ours, a daughter-of-our-hearts, from France, who had been working on a postdoc at the university closest to our former home, had urged us to attend her celebration. We did, and, as is our norm, we cried; the two of us take important transitions very seriously.

A new wife is a new life. A new life is a Yom Kippur, a time of freshness and of aspirations. The moment of marriage is not only a clean slate, per se, but is also vital to living fully. We bless each other that our children should grow to Torah, to the wedding canopy, and to good deeds. When kids are small, they can begin with Torah and with good deeds. Only when they are older ought they to approach the wedding canopy.

Computer Cowboy and I are grateful when we get to participate in others' weddings. Joyously, we run around with those of our friends whose kids are making a new home. We try to help those close ones with their festivity-related chores, we try to provide hospitality to their extended families, and we try to host *Sheva Brachot*. We hold that getting married is a big deal.

Today, it is our turn to celebrate. Mazel Tov!

In a good eye, Missy Older, our oldest child, is engaged. Her groom is a blessing. His family is made up of refined people. There is, as well, a regular and elevated love for Torah in our in-laws' home. My new family configuration is slowly sinking in.

Birthing children pulled me over physical and spiritual thresholds. Birthing a bride lifts me that much higher. My partner and I have never before had a child grow, in a good eye, to the wedding canopy. My new family configuration is slowly sinking in.

I am ecstatic. I am happy. I am grateful to The Name.

I am, as well, having trouble sleeping. My writing spirals in confusing and confounding curlicues. My thoughts start and stop and go neither here nor there. Please bear with me; I'm a little excited.

More broadly, professionally, too, at this moment, I'm guilty of skipping and of begging leave from optional assignments and of getting uncomfortably close to publication deadlines. I'm additionally culpable of approaching writing and editing tasks with a muddled head. My daughter might have taken up temporary residency in Bride Land, but I pitched my tent in La La Land. My new family configuration is slowly sinking in.

The kids formally announced their intentions Thursday night/Friday morning and then, bless them, drove off to the Kotel to daven as an official "bride and groom." Concurrently, though, my family and my husband's family were completing a multi-week trip to Jerusalem, on the occasion of my husband and my 30th anniversary. The last of the three visiting grandparents flew back to the States mere hours before the groom's family met with us to drink *l'chaim,* to life, and to work out "business arrangements." My new family configuration is slowly sinking in.

Older Dude went back to yeshiva the same day as the *L'Chaim,* the first meeting between the bride's and the groom's parents. He is not thrilled about having to travel ten hours, round trip, less than half of a week after settling back into his learning schedule, to attend his sister's forthcoming engagement party. Nonetheless, he plans to be here.

Initially, Missy Younger was excited about fashion options, tableware colors, and other celebration-related details. A few days into this intense period, all the same, she began to bemoan the creative projects she had not been able to complete or to start to actualize given local time constraints. More poignantly, she began to grieve her shifting relationship with her only sister.

Younger Dude, ever level-headed, Bless G-d, has directed his resources toward pointing out that we don't need more posies for our sun porch, that shoes ought to remain practical, and that if someone is needed to taste various caterers' fare, he is willing to offer himself up for such service. He authentically likes his big sister's groom, but wonders, at the same time, aloud, when his mom is going to return to cooking him hot meals and when his father is going to return to taking evening walks with him. My new family configuration is slowly sinking in.

With The Name's help, the engagement party will be tomorrow. Invitations for giving Torah speeches have been issued. Friends have been invited. Someone, yet to be determined, will be in charge of supplying suitable music.

I'm midway through buying paper goods, food, and drink. In stages, I'm also tidying the house.

Yet, I'm torn. While it's important to share festivities, I cherish the moments when my husband, myself, or both of us will again be alone with the new *zug*, couple. Whereas this week, our corner of the world can have dibs on those kids, next week, I am hoping for exchanges that are quieter and more private. My new family configuration is slowly sinking in.

In Jerusalem, where this world touches The World to Come, just as families do elsewhere, families seek halls, apartments, florists, bands, photographers, and the like. Couples pick out furniture, send each other gifts of significance, and fret over towel patterns. Spirituality, even so, remains supreme over materialism in this Holy City, especially during happy occasions.

In being mindful of friends' feelings, trying to accommodate the needs of elderly guests, and always, always, always reminding ourselves and our couple-of-the-hour that their wedding is the springboard to THEIR life, it behooves us to stay focused on what really is important. No one will remember whether or not we had fish or quiche at the celebrations. The bride's flowers will fade. The groom will smile as warmly at the 20th guest as at the 200th. A song, more or less, will not make or break any of the associated parties. On the other hand, remembering where we begin and end, i.e., remembering to give honor to The Highest One, must continue on as quintessential. My new family configuration is slowly sinking in.

The sun has not yet stopped shining in concert with the stars. The air still holds a summer's warmth. Nothing makes sense and, simultaneously, the perfection of all of creation has been, for my family, newly revealed. My new family configuration is slowly sinking in.

Ani L'Dodi V'Dodi Li:
I am My Beloved's and My Beloved is Mine

The King is in the Field. G-d is close to us, at present. We are increasingly aware of the multifaceted nature of the month of Elul. Whether we focus on the processes of employing *t'shuvah,* repentance, *tzedakah,* charity, and *t'fila,* prayer, on averting an evil decree, on The Boss' help in the process of us bettering ourselves, or on our need to engage in interpersonal acts of kindness, we are necessarily busy during this span.

The name of the month of Elul, an acronym for "I am my beloved's, and my beloved is mine," is from a precious verse, specifically 6.3, in *Song of Songs.* Elul's name, like the verse to which it refers, teaches us that we must embrace both *mitzvot bein adam l'makom,* fulfilling our obligations towards our Creator, and *mitzvot adam l'chaveiro,* interpersonal deeds of loving kindness, that we must increase our mindfulness in our relationship to the Highest One concurrent with increasing our mindfulness of our relationships to each other. Even if, during the rest of the year, we lapsed in these areas of self-betterment, Elul brings us a heightened opening in which to adjust ourselves.

First, per Elul's auspicious opportunity to improve our relationship with The Holy One, Blessed be He, we can engage in amends, charity, and prayer. We can also work to better our recognition and appreciation of our eternal partner.

Per the former, the above mentioned, related paths lead us to better incorporate G-d and His ways into our lives. When we emulate Him, we gladden Him.

More specifically, in gladdening The Boss, we show that we recognize the worth of His wonders. In recognizing their worth, we revere The Name as the universe's pinnacle, we pay Him homage. Rabbi Simon Jacobson speaks, in "To Love and Be Loved: Relationships Secrets Unplugged," about the existence of "unconscious resources that we all carry within that allow us to love and be loved,"[23] not the least of which is reconnecting to The Almighty.

However, getting cozier with our Creator is insufficient, specifically, for Elul, and for life, more expansively. We must, as well, build comfort in our human relationships. During this period, it is not enough for us to merely formally wish people well in our correspondence. Rather, we must work on elevating the experiences we share with them.

It is our sins against each other, not any aspect of G-d's loving kindness, which cloud our perception of true reality. In "Sinat Chinam," Rabbi Julian Sinclair writes that "the Talmud infers that groundless hatred is as grave as idol worship, sexual immorality and bloodshed put together."[24] We unquestionably ought to strive to overcome our baseless hatred.

To begin with, we would benefit from understanding that our forgiveness of other people is both possible and necessary. We need to locate and to secure appropriate teachers. We need to pray, pray, pray for the willingness to make changes, and we need to make those changes.

Alternatively, it may be as complex as taking a daily account of our words, our thoughts, and our deeds, and presenting those accounts, for the good of our self-discipline, to trusted others. We'll get no white page in The Name's books as long as our interpersonal behaviors are blotched and stained.

If the aforementioned directives for self-improvement seem too overwhelming, too abstract, or both, think of the allegorical sense of "*Ani L'Dodi V'Dodi Li*," that is, per the building of the *bayit*, the home, of a young groom and bride. Around my home, such analogies are easy as Missy Older continues her preparations for her wedding.

Akin to each Jewish man or woman seeking and finding their soul mate, each Jewish man or woman seeks to improve his or her relationship to The Almighty, even if they do so unwittingly. These connections are determined and are blessed. All that The Name does is just and is for our good. Sometimes, we can more clearly grasp His love than other times. Bless G-d, The Nation of Israel is living during such a time when much of His concern for His beloved flock has been revealed. We know we must lift up our associations with Him and with each other. We know the time to do so is now.

To the Wedding Canopy without Interference

"Marriage." I allow the word to roll around on my tongue. Missy Older is, now, mazel tov, a bride. She has a groom. They are getting married. With the help of Heaven, they will share a life of health, of wealth, and of joy. He is a wonderful young man, Bless The Name! Computer Cowboy and I will be his in-laws.

The twosome's wedding, a Yom Kippur, a Sabbath of Sabbaths, will be a time of extra souls. Their prayers will go faster than average to Heaven as Heaven's gates will be open to them. Those young people, at that time, as well, will be lifted higher than normal off of this world.

Back down on Earth, the rest of us will continue to experience those children's journey as having gone by remarkably quickly. We will, for example, remember, specifically, when Missy Older was born. We will remember that our home-birthed dear one took roughly forty-eight hours to enter this world. We will remember that she bestowed upon us the blessing of becoming "Mommy" and "Daddy," that she transformed us from a couple to a family.

We will bring to the fore, too, recollections of her subsequent adventures, almost all of which became additional "family firsts." She crawled, walked, spoke, and crayoned shortly before Older Dude joined our scene and long before Missy Younger or Younger Dude even glimmered as possibilities in our familial reality.

She learned the "*Shema*," the Jewish confession of faith, first. She went to school first. She became, in the eyes of Torah, at twelve, an adult first.

Interestingly, every time Missy Older shifted developmentally, Bless G-d (growing out of clothes and out of dependencies, alike, are blessings), we, her mom and dad, had to adjust the ways in which we guided her. For this newest change, too, we need to make modifications in our parenting. Mostly, we have to step aside whenever our daughter makes dumb choices.

Whereas it is morally proper to point out dangerous or destructive options, whether those problems loom for individuals, or for people with whom individuals interact, it is poor aid, especially as kids grow up, to point out potential consequences of foolish decision-making. It's tough to jump from heights if you don't yet know how to fly, intuitively or through practice. It's as tough to build a home if you haven't yet discovered your voice and found ways to be comfortable using it. Part of attaining skills is failing.

Applying make-up, fixing a car engine, understanding *Gemara*, commentary on the *Mishnah*, i.e., commentary on the oral tradition of Jewish law, learning compassion, mending socks, baking brownies, washing windows, building a kosher sukkah, knowing when to ask formal questions and when not to ask them, all come with practice. As Jews, we are bid to neither add nor subtract from the ways of Torah. That success, too, comes with experience.

Whereas parents ought to make food choices for their toddlers, they would be foolish to do so for their twenty year-olds. Whereas parents ought to guide their boys and girls in modest words and deeds, they would be foolish to interfere with young marrieds' choices of garments or with their decisions about verbal revelations.

We need to live our dreams, not to impose them on our children. Sharing values is not the same as telling our grown kids what to do. By the time of the wedding canopy, parents are obliged to shut up and to step back. In the least, we want the next generation to sagaciously raise our grandchildren. The cost of such wisdom is their exercising their own critical and creative thinking. It remains okay to cheer them on from the sidelines, though.

Fortunately, The Name gives each of us an entire lifetime in which to grow. Fortunately, He stands by us as we cartwheel on metaphorical balance beams, spotting us so we don't get hurt (unless we're supposed to "experience pain" as a means of learning), and administering to our needs if difficulties, G-d forbid, have to occur. Why would our Father in Heaven do any less for our kids?

My family's new *zug*, new couple, around whom much bustle in both homes full of parents and of siblings is centering, will, with The Name's help, build a *bayis neeman biyisrael, ubinyan adei ad*, a faithful home in Israel, an everlasting edifice and a channel through which to receive G-d's blessings, in all of their material and spiritual needs. The best help we older folks can give them is to encourage, but not to intervene with, their progress. We need to trust that, in partnership with The Boss, they will be fine.

Caterpillars to Butterflies

I knew a small child that had "befriended" a fuzzy caterpillar. She fed it the right sort of leaves for its species, adjusted the temperature in the environment in which she had placed it, kept that space free of predators, and staunchly safeguarded it from her always curious and sometimes destructive pals and siblings.

One day, though, her caterpillar went missing. It had not run away in search of food. It had not fled seeking warmth. It had not been snatched up by unhesitant critters or by malicious humans; the girl had successfully protected and nurtured it. Rather, the little crawler had been replaced by a chrysalis.

Older and wiser people told the grieving child that the juvenile, about whom she had been passionate, had been able to morph to its next natural stage because of her care. Having no better way of framing her hurt, she accepted their words and allowed herself to feel both sad and proud, in waves and mountains, whenever she visited the pupa that had once been her beloved.

Time passed. The girl's former ministrations remained useless to her dear one. She continued on helpless to impact the days and nights of its new phase of development. To intervene would be to harm.

More time passed. One afternoon, something the girl had never before seen emerged from her darling's encasement. That creature had legs, but also wings, hunger, but also flight. It lit on the edge of its habitat box and then, in a revealed miracle, flew away.

The child was stunned and aggrieved. She wept the horror of her loss. In turn, she exclaimed the wonder of her adored one's metamorphosis.

Butterflies have less loyalty than do dumpster cats. To wit, the child never saw her friend again. She did, however, understand, every time she praised G-d for a butterfly, or for a moth, for a bird, for a frog, for a dog, or for a pony, that it is a privilege to behold any aspect of the wonders of the cosmos.

All of us are children. Our Father in Heaven allows us to have intense experiences so that we might grow.

Guiding a child, from an arranged marriage, to her engagement party, and then to the wedding canopy is one such intense experience. Guiding a child from an arranged marriage, to her engagement party, and then to the wedding canopy is a blessed process which necessarily evokes a series of changes, which subsequently, necessarily causes gaps.

Consider that the last time this Jewish mama had trouble sleeping was when something else wonderful happening; my family, Bless G-d, immigrated to Israel. Although I manifested gratitude in prayer, in writing, and in conversations, all of my ordinary, nocturnal connections to The Holy One, Blessed be His Name, and to The World to Come eluded me.

I didn't suffer, though; my inner darkness was illuminated by many candles, all lit by my authentic joy. Such was my experience and such has been my experience, repeatedly, of bereavement, over the last few weeks, ever since my daughter and her groom announced their intentions.

On the one hand, whenever our new family configuration sinks in a bit more, I feel the energy of youth (even though I've been skimping on sleep). On the other hand, concurrently, whenever our new family configuration sinks in a bit more, I feel the fatigue of age (even though The Highest One has not and will not leave my side in our shared project of parenting His children).

All that we parents ever want for our children, in my humble opinion, is to have the chance to properly nurture and protect them so that they will have the chance to evolve through all of the normal and natural stages of life. Most of us neither try to create replications of ourselves or to live vicariously through our offspring. We like our caterpillars to be caterpillars and we strive to accept our butterflies as butterflies.

Since forcing our children to assume unnatural forms is both pointless and destructive, that is, is antithetical to sound guiding, like the aforementioned caterpillar keeper, when our sons and daughters grow up, we exclaim as well as cry.

Suddenly, I comprehend why a friend barricaded herself in her bathroom, for entire weeks, to lament her oldest son moving on, as well as away to a yeshiva high school. These days, I get the gist of the feelings of the pal who wore a mourner's face during the four long years when her middle daughter lived in a far away land, so that the daughter's husband could receive a specialized education.

Not all anguish comes from bad things. Severe pain makes us pay attention; it reminds us that the experience we are undergoing is important. I told my bride that most often hurt, itself, does not break us, but refocuses us. Childbirth, for instance, is the most powerful sensation a human can undergo. Childbirth, as well, is that rarest of opportunities, is that occasion when we partner with The Name in the identifiable miracle of transitioning a soul to this world.

Analogously, witnessing my daughter blossom, Bless G-d, in a good eye, from "young lady" to "bride" is wonderful. This journey *must* call forth deep ache. After all, I hoped and prayed that she would be granted her chance to become a butterfly. I hoped and prayed that I would be granted the wisdom to care for her properly on route to that outcome.

I just never released that her metamorphosis would happen so soon (any time is too soon for a mother). I similarly never grasped what doing "a good job" as a parent might mean.

Passages

Whereas I have not yet morphed into a little Jewish grandmother, who is: capable of using her elbows in the outdoor market, adept at calmly *davening*, praying *Psalms* amidst children throwing taffy, and skilled in harrumphing unfair prices quoted by cabbies, I am evolving, nonetheless. One is never too old or otherwise too far gone to be nudged to new levels of challenge. My children's growth attests to the contrary.

According to the experts populating my household, learning new aptitudes is tough. Falling impacts more than the soft parts onto which we land. Those most delicate moments, especially when generated by our kids, need to be answered with care. Responses that might bring about major upheavals in our sons and daughters' sense of equanimity remain undesirable.

For example, if my stressed out bride dumps on me because, to her, Mommy still feels like the safest person in the universe, I must not snap in answer. Rather, I need to reinforce my boundaries and remind her of all of the good communication skills of which she is possessed.

Similarly, if her younger sister tantrums, I would do well to recall that teenagers lack the social toolboxes that are taken for granted by adults, and that my little one's having to suddenly separate from the only other female child in our home is a tough transition. That is, compassion, not stringency, is the reply I ought to offer.

Furthermore, when my younger sons shrugs and retreats to his room, having mouthed that "at least" his big sister is getting hitched, in that case, too, I am well advised to react by paying close attention to my parental responsibilities; my son and I are both well served if, rather than figuratively throwing my hands heavenward in frustration, or, feeling pushed against a wall, getting literally grumpy in his direction, I invite my child to articulate all of his feelings and I persuade him, or work with him to discover the happiness that is part of our new situation.

Perhaps, my younger son can immediately accept my offer. Perhaps not; the next hour or the next day, likewise, are good times for him to realize the positive in a confusing circumstance. Transitions might be tough on grownups, but they are that much more difficult for adolescents.

What's more, during this time, when the forthcoming celebration is spinning our familial energies, as the mom, I need to help my kids contextualize these changes. Marriage is a big deal. Additionally true is that, at the same time, other vital movements have not stopped taking place. The bride's siblings' conversions might not "sound" as loud as does her metamorphosis, but they are of equal importance. My husband and I, no matter how preoccupied we have become with the approaching wedding, must carry on being our other offsprings' parents.

For instance, another important transformation on the horizon is our older son's entrance into the IDF. Although that event is scheduled for around Purim, it already feels big. That occasion ought to feel big; it is significant. Our older boy will be the first member of our family to experience army. He deserves (as does his bride sister and as do his younger siblings) 100% of his mom and dad's attention.

In addition, that son is to be entering the service during a time when political hot potatoes are getting tossed around the Middle East. While he trusts in The Name, his working as diligently as possible towards achieving a goal includes his knowing what is being asked of him. A lot is being asked of him. Per his major test of faith, my mantra to him, to myself, and to the rest of our family is that The Boss never sleeps and that The Boss protects and favors The Nation of Israel. May The Name protect all of the soldiers in the IDF!

Then there's the New Year. On the one hand, we're supposed to be in the business of making amends on a daily basis. On the other hand, the High Holy Days help us focus on our self-development. Without distractions like work, school, and other worldly matters, the High Holidays gift us with an exceptional opportunity to look at and to improve our connection to G-d.

Correspondingly, these days endow us with an exceptional opportunity to look at and to improve our connection to other people. We are awarded a heightened awareness not only of *mitzvot bein adam l'Makom*, commandments between man and his Maker, but also of deeds of loving kindness between man and his fellow man.

To wit, "being there" for one of our children is insufficient; we need to fully parent *all* of our children. Consider that no matter the pain or elation any one of us feels, The Holy One, Blessed be He, continues to be available to each and every one of the rest of us. Death, unemployment, infertility and

150

other horrendous hurdles do not diminish the suffering of members of the worldwide Jewish community faced with illness, underemployment, or secondary infertility. We need not have the most extreme-seeming challenge in our lives to feel our Father in Heaven's consideration.

We Jews are supposed to emulate the Highest One. We're supposed to encourage all of our kids to seek access to us no matter how important the issues in their lives are, relative to the importance of the issues in the lives of their siblings. My bride has a home and future to think about. My Torah student has army enrollment. My two younger children's current growth opportunities, though, are no less important, just different from those of their siblings.

Moreover, just as The Almighty takes pleasure from our goings-on, we need to remember to take pleasure from the goings-on of our children. We can glean overt and hidden beneficence from their thoughts, words, and deeds if only we make the effort to uncover and, more so, to cherish all of the varied aspects of their souls. Surely, after 120 years, we don't want to have to explain to The Boss why we failed to garner all of the riches available to us through those lovely conduits for joy, to which we gave birth.

Transitioning

It's seeping in. The changes in my nuclear family are slowly ebbing into my awareness. My older daughter is moving out in less than a fortnight; Bless G-d, she's getting married!

On the one hand, whereas children are a large, integral part of one's existence, if one is so blessed (my husband and I gave this daughter, our first child, the middle name "*Nasia*," from the Hebrew word for "miracle," because there had been reasons why we had not been certain we would be accordingly blessed), they are not the totality of one's life. People continue on, with or without children. Consider that we are also possessed of relationships: to G-d, to ourselves, to our partners, to our friends, and to our local and global communities.

Similarly, watermarks, that is, important events, do not constitute the entirety of our lives. Day to day happenings, comprised of the choices we make every few minutes or every few hours, such as whether to wake up on time, or not, whether to pray slowly or quickly, and whether to eat a healthy breakfast, an unhealthy breakfast, or no breakfast at all, are at least as important to us as are our lives' singular moments. Likewise, we are impacted by the ways by which we actualize our choices. For instance, do we live mindfully or mindlessly, do we try to improve our character traits or not, and do we take into consideration the bearing of our actions on other folk, or do we ignore the influence we have on them?

Regardless of how that complex design, which we call "existence," is formed by the relative patterning of special moments within ordinary times, it remains, wonderfully, the case that my oldest child is getting married! This is the initial "parenting of marrieds" event for my husband and for me. Thus, we are living through the array of emotions that accompany such goings-on, *plus* we are living through the array of emotions that surround such goings-on when those goings-on take place for the first time. Whereas I grasp that feelings tend to take on superlative attributes when they are initially owned—that is, when they are first experienced—I nonetheless remain overwhelmed by all of the input currently pouring into my psyche. A sensation of being beset is not necessarily a bad consciousness, yet it is fullness.

In comparison, recall when you became Bat or Bar Mitzvah. Think on your first *shidduch*, arranged marriage, date. Reflect on your own wedding, or on the birth of your first child. Likely, you will agree with me that we individuals are more proficient and less anxious by the second, third, or twentieth time that we undergo any dynamic span.

Sadly, we are also, at least a tad, less awed during subsequent occurrences. I don't believe it is so much that we are jaded, when we re-encounter life's punctuations, as it is that in re-encountering them, we receive smaller tests of our faith and so feel less of a cosmic tug. Usually, during a second, third, or twentieth exposure to a happening, we have at least a vague notion of what to expect. Not so, the first time.

In the case of our daughter's forthcoming nuptials, no matter how many books my husband and I read, no matter how many advisors we seek, no matter how much unsolicited counsel we receive, fear will necessarily find more of our spiritual pores than it will when we, with G-d's help, go through later repetitions of the same happiness with our other children. Correspondingly, any faith we materialize during this time, our virgin experience of a child getting married, is that much purer than it can be during subsequent times.

For perspective, reflect on your first day of school, recall your first time in a swimming pool, remember your first opportunity to participate in public speaking, and think back on the first time you signed for a loan for a house or for a car. All of those occurrences had great potential to end well. All of those occurrences, simultaneously, were difficult. At such junctures, we have to trust.

Because we are not automatons and because The Name and His kindness are not literally palpable, we hope important events end well, especially the first time we proceed through them, but we cannot know beforehand that they will. We have no means by which to guarantee outcomes. Quite the opposite is true; the bigger our investments of our resources, of our time, of our money, or of our strength, often, the more we ache for our experiences to go smoothly.

Since we can't, by ourselves, secure results, we tend to reach to The Almighty. We get what we are supposed to have, which is not always what we want. Sometimes, our results are better than hoped for; sometimes, they are not.

So, points of anguish become points of joy. What seems real proves to be illusionary. We feel, in unequal and unpredictable measure: despair, ecstasy, hopelessness, and elation. We're supposed to: accept rod and staff, like we accept sweetness and light; The Infinite raises us.

I've never married off a child before. I don't know how to do so. My plan, hence, is to gather up all of the benevolence given to me, sing gratitude for it, and imperfectly enjoy my child's celebration.

Her Striped Bathrobe

As my family approaches our oldest child's wedding canopy, I think about the transformations our family is undergoing. There are many.

For me, the most profound differences come from the small matters that make up daily living, such as not being able to continue to witness our big daughter, adorned in her striped bathrobe, at the table, on the sofa, or walking our halls. Additionally, it's already been the case, this year, that after Yom Kippur, after that child and her next older sibling, our nineteen year-old son, snapped together (in Israel, sukkah construction resembles that of Tinker Toys construction) the frame and attached the fabric walls of our *sukkah,* of our hut, rather than joining our family in our post Yom Kippur "second dinner" (we don't eat much more than soup after fasting, for health reasons, and then satisfy our physical hunger later, with omelets or the like), she scurried away with her plate to our sun porch to then attach our sukkah's *s'chach*, the organic material constituting a sukkah's roof. Her groom (who, incidentally, had no part of our omelets having eaten a more traditional break-the-fast before arriving at our home) was waiting on our rooftop patio to help her. Shucks, she didn't even stay around for green pepper or parsley!

I will also miss the business of her method of "making muffins." Missy Older begins by assembling mixing bowls and measuring implements, flour, a flour sifter, baking soda, baking powder, chips, fruit, nuts, seeds, eggs, and rice beverage (our milk substitute), and whatever other foodstuff or equipment she thinks she might need. She then lines tins, pours batter into cake pans, preheats our oven and, eventually, presto chango… pulls warm, almost healthy, yummies out of our appliance. A large percent of those goodies get scarfed down by our family before those treats adequately cool.

It's not her baking that I will miss, though, but her related messes. That child does not enjoy cleaning up as much as she does fashioning desserts. When she moves out, our kitchen will be unnaturally tidy.

I think my husband will miss that aspect of our daughter, too. Albeit, when she lives in her own abode, my husband will no longer have regular access to banana bread, to sunflower seed and pomegranate seed muffins, or to spelt challah (I don't bake), but, more importantly, he will no longer enjoy seeing our oldest child smile mischievously when he calls her out on leaving flour on the counter, utensils in the sink, and bits and things all over the table. He is glad we will be walking her to the wedding canopy, but he will definitely miss her.

Younger Dude is less certain that the forthcoming change is good (nonetheless, he bespeaks it as inevitable). Mostly, our almost 15 year-old sulks as he goes around the house. In addition, he is spending a lot more time than usual in his room. He and our oldest have a special bond. From the time that she helped with his diapers, read him stories, waited for him during family outings when other siblings ran ahead, to now, when they share jokes, hand signals, plus other exclusive forms of relating, she and he have been close. When he was small, our younger son thought everyone had a mom, a dad, and an older sister, such was the connection between those two kids. Even today, he thinks he's best attached to his big sister, as opposed to his sole brother or to the sister who is the sibling closest to him in age. Whereas this son knows that people grow up and move on, and whereas he likes his sister's groom, he's not too keen on watching his big sister leave.

Another take on the entire scenario of our family's transformation is that of our older son. Older Dude, after all, is "cool." Nothing fazes him. Almost nothing. A yeshiva friend, a year older than him, was killed by a terrorist last week (May that terrorist's nation wither, immediately. May the Name avenge all innocent Jewish blood). As per his sister moving out, he will miss her, even though all that he says, publicly, is: that he won't be home, at any rate, to feel the loss, that his father will gain a home office, that he is physically larger than his future brother-in-law, that it will be up to him to pick up the slack in kids' chores when he visits, that he'll be living closer to the newlyweds' city than to ours, and similar such mutterings. Yup, he's grieving.

Missy Younger is a special case, all together. Seventeen, she demands her parents' awareness. She must be immediately compensated for the piece that is sliding away, i.e., for her impending permanent separation from her only sister. She communicates her loss in an age-typical way: slamming doors, using provocative language/bringing up confrontational topics, and, in general, seeking attention for any reason, including less-than-desirable ones. Although she eagerly anticipates moving on and out to *Sherut Leumi*, Israeli National Service, next year, that change will be less difficult for her than is this one for she will be gaining a large measure of independence. This year, in contrast, she sees herself as suffering a deficit.

I smell schnitzel burning in the kitchen. I hear young voices arguing about whose turn it is to empty the garbage cans. I hear my spouse asking why no one is helping him truck all of the cases of water, which he bought for Sukkot, up our few flights of stairs. For now, my entire immediate family is living under the same roof. We still have a little time to adjust to the forthcoming metamorphosis.

Bridal Sabbath

The girlies are coming! The girlies are coming! In two days' time, a magnificent, energized coterie of young women will descend upon my home, will pull food out of my pantry and refrigerator, will otherwise take over my kitchen, and will cause songs to ribbon from their mouths. Those guests will pitch their sleeping bags throughout my rooms, will festoon my saloon with their games, will read aloud from letters specifically collected for the occasion, will engage in many other antics (none of which, of course, will break any of the rules of Sabbath observance), and will stay up far too late with my already exhausted daughter. They will push the boundaries of bedtime in order to tell stories about and to her, and they will joke with her. All of this forthcoming chaos will be wonderful; it will be my child's Bridal Sabbath.

Before the event, we will cook together. Whereas one of my friends is generously making enough cake to feed twice the number of young women arriving for our special Sabbath, there remain other preparations; we have quiches to bake, chicken to sauce, and lots of veggies and salads to chop. What's more, we have Torah speeches to compose and blessings to organize. Torah, after all, elevates Sabbath.

In addition, the forthcoming event constitutes another reminder that less than a week remains before I walk, with my husband and my daughter, to my daughter's wedding canopy. That child of ours, the one who elected to live at home during her *Sherut Leumi,* National Service, year and during all of the years of college that she has thus far completed, is embarking on a new portion of her journey. Her future configuration is just starting to hit her. She is freaking out.

On the one hand, her groom, Bless G-d, is a wonderful young man. She and he, in a good eye, seem very happy together. I believe they will grow closer and more mature, over time, because of the goodness of their bond. As well, each of them will continue on in the studies in which they are already successfully engaged. They will move, too, to a community where they, individually, and through either of their sets of parents, have

158

wonderful friends. The daily basics are, Bless G-d, in a good eye, already in place for them. There is much for which to be grateful.

Yet, because my child is transitioning, I find myself, several times a day, reassuring her that she is not lost to us. Rather, we are expanding our nuclear family to include her husband. Then, I wink and suggest that maybe we'll merit gaining, over the next few years, a few grandchildren, too.

Despite this encouragement from me, suddenly, there are not enough hugs or back rubs, for her, from Mommy, and not enough walks and long talks, for her, with Daddy. This daughter can't make enough minutes materialize out of the ether to spend with any of her siblings, either.

So, my family continues to comfort her. As Jews, we are taught to keep in mind that "this, too, shall pass." Any moment, no matter the amount of solace or pain it holds, is transitory. Yet, children seem to be oblivious to the preciousness of each segment of life. Adults, maybe, begin to appreciate, and to hold, perhaps, the fact of the fleeting quality of our seasons. It is understandable that big events raise awareness in ways in which mundanities cannot.

As a soon-to-be wife, my daughter is awakening to her new stage of living. She is beginning to grasp the value of human relationships and is beginning to appreciate all of the good that has filled her life. It's of little wonder that she returns, again and again, for more hugs.

As for me, I do best during dynamic times when I lock myself in a given day. Sometimes, I struggle so much I need to grasp life by hours or by minutes.

For now, I volley phone calls and emails about my daughter's Bridal Sabbath, juggle grocery lists for the same, and reflect on which of our tableside prayer books have Sabbath songs in them. The tea lights are ready for the many hands that will be *benching lecht,* saying the blessing over the Sabbath candles, this last of my daughter's Sabbaths at home, as a single girl. I've ordered challot.

Female relatives are emailing in snips and bits about the bride's childhood. Last minute reminders are going out to each young visitor to bring her own linens (I am not washing over a dozen sets of sheets—in fact, I don't even own that many sets—days before a wedding). My family is almost there, is nearly at the point where we wish the bride well amidst songs and prayers, is approaching that juncture in time and space where we hand her off, so to speak, to her new husband.

Meanwhile, I've bought pretty napkins and colorful, disposable serving vessels. I've asked my younger children to distract the bride, outside of our home, the night and the morning her friends and I are preparing her Sabbath party. I've also cried and cried.

Wedding Countdown

I have read the books, have sought a "reasonable" amount of advice, and have been given so much information, beyond the aforementioned, by well-intended persons, that I could create celebrations for dozens of brides and grooms. However, I won't. I will, instead, focus on what is in front of me.

Blissfully, my family is days away from our older daughter's nuptials. In a word, our house is chaos, happy chaos. The phones ring. Emails arrive unrelentingly. Friends, who are tired of my family's electronic bottlenecks, now, instead, literally knock on our door (in our neighborhood, no one knocks on doors). Most days, three to five different sets of people knock on our door. Bless G-d, our dear ones are as excited about the upcoming joyous day as are we.

Our child, who lived at home during her *Sherut Leumi* year, and during all of the college years that she has thus far completed, is suddenly realizing that her wedding canopy will bring not only the gain of her husband, but also the loss of her dwelling in the only emotional home (shifting geographies don't count) that she has ever known. This realization overwhelms her.

It overwhelms me, too. For the moment, I am electing to compartmentalize that thought. After the week of *sheva brachot*, celebratory meals featuring the seven blessings, I believe I'll have time to process this realization. Such contemplation deserves a greater quantity of my temporal resources than I currently have available.

I don't expect to have similar needs to sort out my feelings with my second and third children. They have already "been away," respectively, at *hesder yeshiva*, yeshiva that includes army service, (I only cried for two weeks leading up to that separation) and during summers for camp. The camper, what's more, plans on spending her *Sherut Leumi* time first in a distant city and then, for a second year, somewhere else in the world. Neither of those children, nor I, will experience the dissonance the current bride and I are feeling, at present.

As per what my youngest will do, there's no telling how that separation will evolve; like my oldest, to date, he's chosen to live at home. He's only in ninth grade, though, so he and I still have plenty of preparation time before he joins with a wife.

The background emotional commotion in my home notwithstanding, my family's down to the nitty-gritty. We are attending to last minute details. Gifts are being bought for our nightly house sitters (sadly, in the Holy City, criminals tend to prey on families who are away from their homes for weddings, for *sheva brachot*, and for any other publicly known happy occasion), professional manicures (a first for all of the ladies in my family) are being ordered, and some small amount of thought is being given to what to feed our sons during the celebratory week, a time when parties will leave the daughters and the parents wanting not to contemplate food, but will leave the sons opening and reopening the refrigerator door in search of meals.

Beyond experiencing anxieties and responding to relative minutia, my family is also tripping up a bit. Even when we grasp that this season, for us, is necessarily one of delight, and even when we grasp that true cosmic ecstasy undergirds our countenances at this time of the building of a new Jewish home, my family still has to deal with our personal and collective embodiments of the evil eye.

Accordingly, no matter the rarity of the phone calls of congratulations from Europe or from North America, we still go through momentary despondency. No matter the extent to which local friends give of themselves to raise our joy, we still encounter the dispatched darkness that masquerades as reality. No matter the giggles, tears, or other shared feeling passed among us, we still repeat the mistake of being disheartened, i.e., of wrongly releasing ourselves to shadowy thoughts.

In remedy, my family places ourselves in environments full of Torah. A span with increased amounts of attention to materialism is a span that requires increased amounts of attention to *ruchnius*, to spiritual matters. Now, a time when we are vulnerable because of our elation, we absolutely must surround ourselves with people of good character traits, with books of Torah and Torah commentary, and with acts of loving kindness.

Fortunately, Torah is water, which is a substance that can, over time, erode even stone. Little by little, this moisture, and all else that is nurturing, trickles into my family's beings even if we don't deserve such gifts, even if we fall on our faces from error during a time when we could, alternatively, be raising our souls. Fortunately, The Name will never stop Loving us.

His light necessarily permeates our darkness; such is the nature of the universe. Even when we intentionally block our souls' apertures, light returns to us. Even when we purposefully seal ourselves away in unnatural environments, spiritual sustenance finds us. Even when we hide the better portions of our souls, G-d plants His kisses on us; He continues to fill our days and nights with the best of all pleasant things. Our Father in Heaven necessarily remembers us even when we stray from His prescribed path. It's our duty to notice and to rectify our faults. It is not and never will be our charge to try to be perfect.

It can't matter that we had to make a last minute switch among florists, that one of our children's way of participating in the festivities, so far, has left us wanting, or that another family member's haircut looks a little funny. Our focus ought to be on the opportunity to take a bride to the wedding canopy, to support a *zug*, a couple, in establishing a family, not on worldly matters. Period.

So, during these days, these hours just before the wedding, whether my family, collectively, or individually, acts like angels or like rocks, The Name and His kindness exist, did exist, and will continue to exist beyond any impact we make on local causality. All we can do is to try to do our best and to amend any mistakes that we notice we are making.

The New Normal

In my home, we need to construct a fresh blueprint. Whereas Older Dude, Missy Younger and Younger Dude still use their parents' postal address (albeit Older Dude is on the cusp of moving from his *hesder yeshiva*, yeshiva combined with IDF service, to solely the IDF service, and albeit Missy Younger is looking into national and into international options for next year's *Sherut Leumi*, National Service), Missy Older has gone and gotten married.

On the one hand, I am grateful my older daughter found the person who will complement her perfectly. On the other hand, I miss her much more than a lot.

It's not so much that she was tied, at the umbilicus, to me, as it is that she is my firstborn. Her first loss of a baby tooth was monumental, as was her first day at school. Her first sleepover at a friend's home was reason enough to ring up the entire extended family, and the first Sabbath during which she filled our home with her friends felt like reason enough to sing "*Hallelukiah*," "Hallelujah."

It follows that when this first of my offspring moved to her own nest, that event, her big transition, felt epic to me. Sure, it's best when life's significant moments are palpations of good things. Better a wedding than a funeral. Better a nice Jewish boy than an evil son of who-knows-who. Nonetheless, feelings of leave-taking wash over me in ways for which I had failed to prepare. I doubt people are equipped, in actuality, to prepare for such matters.

More than the crumbs left on my family's dairy sandwich maker, more than the laundry left unsorted in front of our washing machine, and more than any email imploring me to "quickly" respond to some problem of documentation or of diction (the bride's determined to create and to teach text, just like her Mom), there are other, more significant, trails left behind. For the moment, those unspoken words, those unreceived hugs, and all of those other unactualized tokens of our relationship feel like avenues of emptiness.

Late at night, when I am wrestling with my next best jumble of words, there is no little blond head peering into my office asking why I am still awake. Early in the morning, when I am blearily stumbling toward the shower, there is no slim chick competing for the hot water. These days, when I prepare to greet the Sabbath Queen, there is no twenty-something thanking me for teaching her how to cook, while simultaneously asking me to leave the kitchen to her since she likes her version of certain recipes better than she likes mine.

As a mother-daughter unit, we invested in seemingly countless whispered conferences, on our living room sofa, about whether or not she ought to date a certain lad, about whether or not she ought to continue to date a different fellow, and about whether or not she ought to accept the marriage proposal of the one she loves. All such issues are moot, now. There is no more need for furtive meetings. There is no longer a younger partner with whom to speak.

What's more, there are no new topics to replace those precious sharings; according to my sensibilities, newlyweds ought to be left alone. So, I don't call and I certainly don't visit.

That daughter of mine knows how to find me by email (I still loathe texting and despise IM'ing) if she has a domestic or scholarly question. As per items of the interpersonal nature, it's probably not any longer appropriate to consult Dear Old Mom.

So, I breathe a new normal, glad that I've helped to equip my oldest child, that sweet young lady, with resources and with the ability to seek answers when her personal means prove insufficient. Yet, that happiness of mine is threaded with sadness; one of my roles, in terms of that particular child, is over. I have, in one regard, fortunately, become obsolete. Suddenly, I feel my chronological age.

In balance, my life, Praise G-d, remains full of blessing. I maintain the status quo in my relationships with: my husband, my other children, my extended family, my friends, members of my synagogue, and my professional associates. I still wipe dust from our living room's bookshelves, I still rub my spouse's back when he is tense, I still worry over my younger daughter's nail polish, I still pray for my older son's army placement to be favorable, and I still wonder about my younger son's ability to pack away comestibles. As well, there remain the friends who need cheering, whom I call, and the newbies who need a hand up, whom I try to humbly assist. Life goes on, irrespective of the changes I undergo.

Nevertheless, for now, at the end of each day's cycle, I grieve. It was through the creation of my oldest child that I became a parent. With G-d's help, in the future, she will make me a grandparent and, possibly, even a great-grandparent. Already, this oldest offspring has made me a mother-in-law. Already, she has made me lonely.

No More Vegetarian Sabbaths

In my home, there will be no more regular consideration of how to add a vegetarian element to Sabbath. You see, my local avoider of meat, fish, and poultry got married and moved away.

It used to be the case, when planning cholents, chops, roasts, and liver, I also had to think about the preparation of parve quiches, tofu stir-fries, and kindred dishes. Simple, but Sabbath-appropriate recipes needed to be included on behalf of my fair-haired child, who would pet a chicken, but not eat one.

Over the years, such mindfulness amounted to keeping lentils, beans, nuts, seeds, and high-intensity grains in stock. Whereas my awareness ought to have also included, during those rare Sabbaths, when we were guests (we prefer, in my family, to stay home and to welcome guests more than we seek to be visitors), a mention that one among us was disinclined to eat dead critters, I usually forgot.

Such diligence is moot these days. Not only do I not need to preview, for hosts, the fact that one of my children won't touch flesh, but I also don't need to reshape my own preparations. Missy Older doesn't live with us any more. I miss her.

Per a certain point of view, I can contextualize my loss by remembering that my life features not only the wonky protagonist, who is me, but, additionally, other riotous characters, namely my husband and my children. They share my shortfall.

Missy Older was known for her striped bathrobe. Recently, Missy Younger took over ownership of that garment, took on responsibility for that one among many possessions, which Missy Older intentionally and symbolically left behind upon shedding her childhood for the womanhood that comes with marriage.

This past *Motzi Shabbot*, night after Sabbath, while Missy Younger was culling comfort from that well worn wrap, both of her brothers, during separate moments, did a double take upon entering our salon and seeing Missy Younger in that striped robe. Neither boy realized that the bathrobe's ownership had been transferred. More exactingly, each thought, on viewing the younger of their two sisters from behind, as improbable as it seemed, especially since Missy Older and her new husband, less than an hour earlier, had left their first post-wedding canopy Sabbath with us, that somehow Missy Older, in her former incarnation, had returned home. My sons suffer.

Consider, too, the post-wedding plight of my poor, old husband. While I take comfort from literally crying my losses on our sofa, or from pretending that no family member can hear me weeping in my anything-but-soundproof office, the strong impact of this change, as made manifest in my dearest one, gets ignored. Granted, there is a lot more mellow, even somber, acoustic guitar music wafting up the staircase, originating from his work, than wafted up before, and granted his interest in taking walks, playing Scrabble, in doing just about anything with our other children has phenomenally increased. Yet, none of us have invited him to put his leaking feelings to words. He, too, is ailing from this passage.

Per a different point of view, I can argue that no one can possibly grasp, except, of course, other mothers, what a transformation in a child's status means to her female parent. Mommies gestate, nurse, and otherwise lend their bodies and their inner beings to their babies. We literally hold their hands on the playground and in the school yard and figuratively lend them support through the excruciating steps of *shidduchim*, the matchmaking process. Mother-child relationships are unique. Changes to them are distinctively felt by mothers.

No matter whether the other members of my family endure this experience equally, or mine is the great portion of deficit, all of us want Missy Older to be happy. Ultimately, parents want children to establish their own homes. Ultimately, siblings want partners for each other. We have no idea what we are praying for.

My sons took turns telling me, during the last few years, how important it was for their older sister to find a spouse. My younger daughter thrilled with each date undertaken by my older one and was palpably devastated by each suggested boy that didn't work out. As per my husband, during our child's "meeting and greeting," he mused long and frequently about our own couplehood, which had begun when we were eighteen and which has continued on, thus far, in a good eye, for decades thereafter. He wanted the same thing for Missy Older.

Me? I invested many resources in querying matchmakers, friends, and others toward the end of trying to help our older daughter. I waded through references, asked lots of questions, and stayed up nights, after her dates, trying to help her sort out her feelings. My entire family wanted her to be married since she wanted to be married.

All of us like her husband. In fact, we're entirely grateful that he is in her life and in ours. It's just that Missy Older no longer lives at home.

After the Confetti

At many of the *sheva brachot*, the feasts held after the wedding canopy, which were held for my daughter and my new son-in-law, the bubbles, confetti, and kindred accoutrements that had been made available, were meant to enhance the "fun" tenor of those evenings. Now, days later, fewer and fewer bits of those sparkly appurtenances show up in my family's laundry, in our laundry baskets, and on the floor, in front of our washing machine.

Today, the most interesting small pieces of whatnot found among my family's clothes, in our wash vessels, and on the floor, once more are dust bunnies and twigs. Little glitter remains. In addition, I'm no longer receiving frantic emails about photographers, musicians, hair stylists, or the like. As well, no blond-haired twenty-something is slinking around the halls of our home trying to avoid attention; as of nearly two weeks ago, she resides in her own home.

Her striped robe, though, remains here. Not only did she leave behind her last name, but she also cast aside many sorts of material goods from her original life. Missy Younger snatched up a lot of Missy Older's discarded clothes. I snatched up many of the discarded crafts projects fashioned by Missy Older's fingers. My husband snatched up Missy Older's former bedroom as his new, "proper" home office.

Meanwhile, our collective family life ebbs toward a new normal. Consider that when Younger Dude pokes his head out of his room and surveys our domestic landscape, he returns to his space a tad sullen. His big sister is nowhere to be seen and she will not, except for visits, surprise or planned, dwell in our home again. She's married.

As per Older Dude, who's currently sorting out army choices, he says nothing, but acts as though everything has shifted. It's palpable to us, his other loved ones, just how much he wishes his "twin" (as Missy Older and Older Dude, two years apart in age, were referred to by strangers when they were young) was here so that he could bounce his thoughts against her good judgment. He misses trading iPod tunes with her, too.

Missy Younger slams the door more and more, says I understand her less and less. It's as though some change in family dynamic has morphed our relationship.

As for my help-opposite, he gives over to me all of the jokes he used to share with our daughter. I appreciate the gesture. The ritual, though, is not mine.

It's not so much that my family is in mourning, albeit, a real phase in our shared lives has passed (never again will we be the six of us), as it is that we are traveling a span of commemoration. Remember how Missy Older left the dishes in the sink when the family cooked for Sabbath? Remember how Missy Older huddled with Missy Younger when the boys went off with Dad for *Mincha*, the afternoon prayer service, and *Ma'ariv*, the evening prayer service? Remember how Missy Older would tap on my office door, nearly every *Motzi Shabbot*, just to "check in," just to make sure the world, as she knew it, was still predictable, and, consequently, safe?

I practiced attachment parenting. I birthed the kids at home (except for one whose medical situation required a different venue), nursed them through their toddler years, tried to support their expressions of creativity even when their shared lexis included digging up our lawn (I supplied the shovels) and coloring homework-issued tree tops with purple crayons.

I learned herbal medicine from Susun Weed so that I might be able to provide my little dears with a greater array of responses to their health needs than offered solely by conventional medicine, and became a *Baalat Teshuva*, a returnee to the Torah life, in no small part so that my sons and daughters could tuck into their heritage. When the opportunity to move to Israel came, my husband and I jumped at it for ourselves and, especially, for our children. Then the first birdie flew away.

The ever wise *Shlomo HaMelech*, King Solomon, espoused that "this, too, shall pass." He was advising a troubled soul. In spite of that application of his insight, such astuteness, as we learn in *Ecclesiastes,* applies to seemingly wonderful qualities of life, equally. Raising a child to the wedding canopy, a summit that parents pray for, is a wonderful point in life. Bear in mind that parenting, in the final evaluation, is merely a means of accessing a higher good. Our children, after all, are on loan to us from Heaven. Nurturing them, one hopes, creates routes by which we might achieve our ultimate goals; to fear The Holy One, Blessed be He, and to keep His commandments.

I suppose I will continue to shake out our shirts, skirts, pants, and tzitzis, that is, the ones piled into heaps in my family's laundry, in hope of espying yet one more blue, silver, red, green, or gold spangle. I suppose I will continue to sigh every time I discover the sprinkles left behind in our pantry, by Missy Older, who adored them with her ice cream. I suppose I will continue to run my fingers on the the *seforim*, religious texts, which she left on our salon's shelf, and I suppose I will continue, especially when no one is looking, to hug the outgrown sandal, which she forgot to retrieve from behind our sofa.

Sure, she and I will remain, with G-d's help, in regular communication. I'm open to any stream of calls or emails, from my dear bride, about vegetable soup, about bleaching bathroom floors, or about bus routes to and from her new abode to her school. I'm happy to give her motherly encouragement on time management, on budgeting, and the like. I have no problem with supplying parental discipline, either. It's just that that golden daughter of mine doesn't live here anymore.

Inspiration from Difficulties

As Simple as Holding Open a Door

Life rushes by. One day I was happily putting on my new purple glitter "jelly" shoes for kindergarten, and the next day I was in my cap and gown, graduating from eighth grade. Before I knew it, I was preparing the scenery for my high school's twelfth grade show, and, today, here I am, in *Sherut Leumi*.

Although my life feels as though it has gone by quickly, I never would have gotten to where I am without help. Most of the changes I have made were guided by mentors. I feel as though I usually had someone holding a door open for me as I passed through. My entrances were not always graceful, and sometimes I tried to keep one foot in a previous room, but the pushes I received from my life's teachers, and from their explanations of what could be found behind new doors, often helped my passage.

All of us are presented with doors, daily. Sometimes, we've created them, and sometimes others made them. Either way, the rooms beyond those doors represent the next part of our personal growth. Just because some doors don't have our names on them doesn't mean we can't try to open them. At times, it takes a brick to keep a door open. Other times, heavy baggage helps. Most times, if a door closes, two open. Always, it's useful to try them. In the process of trying them, we might not only find them open, but we might also learn how to choose among them.

Life's easiest paths are not always the best ones. The first openings we find are not always the only ones. Sure, it's scary to go through an unfamiliar portal, but it's better to test the unknown than to get stuck in a room. Life is for living.

— Rivka

Basic human rights and freedoms need not be limited to the workings of government muckety-mucks. Whereas treaties such as the *Magna Carta*, or, more recently, *The Universal Declaration of Human Rights*, sound at once both wonderful and unobtainable, we individuals do have the power to actualize human integrity. Sometimes, reaching this goal can be as simple as holding open a door.

"Doors" can be either literal or figurative. Palpable doors are the barriers we close, mindlessly, when someone else is also trying to enter a building or a room. Whereas such structures are meant to separate, being merely sheaths of wood or of metal, they make no distinction between exclusion and inclusion; it is we, who when charging through our days, forget the needs of the school child, of the elderly man, or of the package-laden messenger, who is walking just a few paces behind us.

We can interfere with "doors" that are symbolic, rather than tactile, too. When we slam a student, shut out a youth, close ourselves to an employee, or otherwise forget that there are degrees of empowerment among the social strata, and that such differences are neither ignored nor unfelt by most persons, we are creating unnecessary gaps amongst ourselves. As individuals who have authority in a given situation, we necessarily also have responsibility for maintaining that portion of our greater social fabric. Freedoms are not something that we can purchase at a neighborhood franchise or that we can limit ourselves to sing about at political rallies; freedoms result from the negotiation of human interactions. Freedoms require constant maintenance.

Even in this era of big promises by big officials, it is the little moments that have the potential to create and to enhance our liberties. The next time that you are monitoring a door, consciously or otherwise, consider holding it open.

— Hannah

Smoldering Dumpsters and Other "Rhetorical Devices"

To get to my Hebrew class, in the heart of New Jerusalem, I can take many routes. If I want to exercise on the way, though, I am limited to three choices: to walk from the outdoor market to my class, to walk along HaNavim Street to my class, or to walk from Sabbath Square to my class. Each way has plusses and minuses. The outdoor market path enables me to grab a hot chocolate from a respectably-*hecshered* vendor, i.e., one with reliable kashrut observance, and to shop thriftily (I can't buy what's not for sale—Israeli ingenuity aside, most stores don't open until 10:00, an hour long past the start of my ulpan). The HaNavim path means I can imbibe joy from watching the college students scampering, half asleep, to one of several institutes of higher learning in that area (once a teacher, always a teacher). The Sabbath Square path means I can immerse myself in a part of the city where residents dress modestly and visitors are admonished to do the same.

On the flip side, the outdoor market path is full of buses, puddles, and smokers. Umbrella rims and extended elbows remain a constant there. The HaNavim path, on the other hand, is less congested. However, that scarcity of pedestrian traffic results, partially, from our genetic cousins' sovereignty there. Recently, the media have reported stabbings, of our people, along HaNavim. As for the path through the Geulah and Mea Shearim neighborhoods, the one that winds through a historic district with charmingly narrow sidewalks, as a rule, I have nothing but praise (though, I feel anxious if one of my knee socks starts to slip). Unfortunately, the other day, this third path, the one I especially cherish when I need a visual and auditory boost of Yiddishkeit, too, presented problems.

Before I discuss the meaning of overturned dumpsters, of garbage-strewn streets, of smoldering rubbish, of broken street signs, and of busted light fixtures, and before I refer, in balance, to the catalyst of this neighborhood's strong outpouring of emotion, to the not yet (at least at the time of this writing) canceled exhibition of public sacrilege, let me clarify the essence of "rhetorical device." A "rhetorical device" is a linguistic component that sacrifices ends, results, or consequences for immediate sensory satisfaction, i.e., language that is beautified, or that is otherwise artificially enhanced, for the purpose of retaining a reader's or listener's attention, but not necessarily for the purpose of infusing conviction in that reader/listener. Think: rock music, college-level classes in the syntax (grammatical structure) of poetry, invitations to New World weddings, and the like. Since linguistic contrivances call out to an audience, yet usually fail to retain an audience's interest, such devices are a lot about noise and only a little about lasting influence.

Regardless, I took the third road because it is winter in the Old World. Winter here is not about the piles of snow and slush indigenous to the New World (physical winter here is rain), but about the feeling that Sabbaths seem to evaporate (I refuse to go along with the parlance that refers to winter Sabbaths as "short;" all Sabbaths have at least twenty-five hours [Younger Dude is still campaigning for us to wait to recite the prayers that close out Sabbath until Tuesday morning, some week; I am still campaigning for more words of faith, more singing, and more whole wheat challot]).

In the summer, afternoon prayers and evening prayers begin after most small children ought to be sleeping (New World friends report that their children are equally as clever as are Israeli youngsters at perpetrating late night antics), the first Sabbath meal is held thereafter, followed by spiritual table talk, singing, a bit of sleep, morning prayers, a second festive meal, learning or a class on holy matters, a nap (New World friends report that their rest periods are equally as necessary as are Israeli ones, given their children's equivalent propensity to create disturbances), a third meal, afternoon prayers, evening prayers, and the prayers that conclude Sabbath. By the time that guests, who are young enough not to need a second slumber party, pack up (those people have neither New World nor Israeli sprouts to which to tend), it's again the small hours. Ahhhhh, summer Sabbaths!

Winter Sabbaths are not so languid (no matter how weighty the cholent or how soggy the humor). After the kids' half day of school and a few scant chores, it's time, at an almost obscenely early hour, to welcome the Sabbath Queen. No little ones are falling asleep between fish and kugel, no middle-sized ones are high from staying up until the "enchanted" hours between ordinary bedtime and ordinary waking, and no older ones have time to be assuaged by a hearty nap. (Do not believe, for even a moment, that this dearth of parental nap time means a lack of opportunity for the antics of the little persons. They have the means. They have the motive. They find the opportunity. Just one parental back turned: to change dishes, to grab a prayer book for a spiritual class, or to extend a welcome to a guest suffices for a mischief-making opening, even in winter.)

Thus, my perception of my Sabbath "deprivation," i.e., of my most recent winter Sabbath, influenced my Sunday morning route through the older neighborhoods. Lamentably, instead of palpable holiness, I got "artificial enhancement."

I am a Jew. I am an Israeli. I am an Israeli Jew/Jewish Israeli, who cannot wait until those two words will, at last, be synonymous. I am of an impassioned people. I love The Boss. I love His Torah. I love doing my humble best to live a life of His Torah. I am grateful for the material things given to me; a place to live, food to eat, clothes to wear. I am grateful for the ability to see, to locomote, to breathe. I am grateful for the spiritual abundance that is Jerusalem. Consequently, I don't understand how leaving so many, and such a variety, of literal stumbling blocks throughout much of two holy neighborhoods, how breaking signs, how creating more "wage earning opportunities" for the relatives of those knife wielders from Rechov HaNavim, or how any other manner of "jumping up and down," of "creating rhetoric flourishes," has the staying power to drive away cultural demons, rather than, sadly, to transform our special streets into additional examples of what's undesirable.

I'm not entirely convinced that by burning garbage, by adding "linguistic embellishments" to the teachings that our religious society diligently aims to uphold, that we are achieving our cause. I winced watching: a cane-supported man walking to his neighborhood prayer gathering sliding in waste; a mother, steering a single-terrain baby buggy loaded with twins, dodging sewage; a shopkeeper overwhelmed by doorstep debris, trying a rake, a hose, and a shovel to clear the way to his livelihood; and a bunch of cute little kids, walking hand-in-hand with even smaller ones, trying to pull themselves over, around, or if need be, through the trash. Maybe the strewn, burnt, water-sodden garbage was meant to symbolize the abomination that stirred the protests. Maybe the strewn, burnt, water-sodden garbage was just a tacit version of aposiopesis, of enallage, of paregmenon, of Wellerism, or of other types of communication that are used to draw attention to a subject usually relegated to somber regard, and hence, maybe regrettably, usually relegated to being overlooked.

In fairness, our government doesn't always listen (plenty of pundits write about this "hearing" problem). In fairness, recent polls indicate a disconcerting amount of hemorrhaging among Jews' attitudes toward each other; just about everyone blames just about everyone else for our social wrongs, but does little to build bridges or to solve problems. In fairness, we are responsible, at some point, for each other's choices, and historically, we have been both punished and rewarded by The Boss, because of the actions of our brethren. Accordingly, I'm not quite sure that adopting a solution of communication, which exploits the nature of interaction, doesn't somehow jeopardize the very foundation of the reality we are trying to preserve and to purify. I hope I am merely missing the (rhetorical) point.

In a day or two (or longer, if this emotional response to a very authentic crisis continues), I'll probably return to the third of my three possible exercise routes to ulpan. I like walking past: religious texts shops, labs for detecting forbidden mixtures of clothing fibers, and Bait Yaakov schools. I like riding the mehadrin bus to Jerusalem's center. I like when our social rhetoric is free of device.

Idiot Drivers and Car Horns

I don't like to give up. Most things, I try until I get them right. Then again, I usually only try things at which I believe I can succeed. When I succeed, it may not be my first try or my second or third, but at least I get to choose what I try.

One thing that I have had no choice about is driving lessons. My parents, who of course "always know best," insisted that I learn the way of the road, in particular, that I learn the way of the road from the driver's seat.

I really didn't want to learn how to drive. In my opinion, it is a huge waste of time and money. But, as I well know, it's hard to argue with parents, who end up being right a lot more then I care to admit. So, I'm now in the midst of driving lessons and theory tests.

Actually, I would have no problem driving if there were no other cars on the road. It would be great not to have to watch out for other drivers passing on the right (right is wrong, right?) or slamming on the brakes when they decide to pull over to a spot that they invented and that is illegal. But that's the reality of driving in Israel; the drivers in Israel are *Israeli*.

Not only do I have problems with the drivers when I drive, they also manage to bother me when I walk. Take, for example, my walk home from school. I used to walk home every few weeks. I have since stopped. It's not the heat that bothers me; sweating is healthy. The distance is fine too; five miles isn't so bad, especially when only half of that length is uphill. Plus, all of those ascensions give me hope that I might, one day, have thin legs. The weight of my backpack (on the days that I decide it's in my best interest to do my homework) isn't that much of a problem, either. But I simply cannot stand THEM. "THEM" are the motorists (and construction workers) who take it upon themselves to honk, to catcall, to whistle, and to otherwise remind me that few women in Israel are natural blonds. I am a natural blond.

That acting has become very annoying to me; in fact, it has gotten to be very offensive to me, very quickly. Now I have no hope for my thighs and a new hatred for other drivers. Not only do I have to watch out for those drivers who decide that red lights are only a suggestion, but I also have to wear a bandanna when I stroll. Validation that my hair is pretty feels nice, but telling it to myself in the morning when I look in the mirror has long been plenty.

On the other hand, another rule I have, per not giving up, is trying to see the good in everything. I figure that there is some way that I can use this unsolicited attention to my benefit. One day, I will discover that it can help me get married.

See, I really want to get married. At the same time, I have all of these people starting up with me. I figure that if the next guy who beeps at me offers to marry me, I'm good, no? Maybe I'll even write one of those signs that hitchhikers have. In the place of "Tel Aviv" or "Jerusalem" I can write "Wedding" or "Marriage." Who knows, something might yet come of it. All I need is a poster board and a magic marker, and I'll be set for life.

— Rivka

Much has been written about the ways and means of Jerusalem's drivers. Pedestrians and motor vehicle operators, alike, take notice of the "creative" way in which most local roadsters navigate most local roads.

In my esteem, this city's car masters are remarkable in their indifference to established and implicit laws. On the one hand they'll stop, mid traffic, to honor the fallen when national sirens sound. On the other hand, they'll drive on curbs, between lanes, and in various additional "inspired" fashions, in order to arrive just a bit faster to that next red light.

Furthermore, many of this city's drivers park in manners that cause damage to their own as well as to their neighbors' cars and trucks, play "bumper tag" in order to change lanes just a bit more quickly, and leave behind evidence, i.e., bits of chrome, plastic, and glass, of their carefree ways, so that other drivers can "enjoy" a little more of that creeping patina known as "wrecks." In short, these same Jerusalem drivers, who compromise their ever cartoon-like jalopies, seem disinterested in driving constraints. "Thoughtlessness" remains their code.

Sometimes, Jerusalem drivers lack inhibition in their relationship with Jerusalem pedestrians. Their rash behavior manifests in their ignoring of school-aged occupants of crosswalks, in their ogling pretty girls out of their passenger-side windows (while still steering), and in their snarking at, or otherwise flailing their cars and their limbs toward perambulators. So wild are these drivers' behaviors that many would-be walkers elect, instead, to forego the health benefits derived from moving about and ride buses instead (ironically, this response is not necessarily safer; bus operators, also, are drivers).

Too often, I hear my children claim: that an elder was run down by a driver preoccupied with shaving his face or with plucking her eyebrows, that a tourist, who actually stopped at a red light, was rear-ended, (in Jerusalem, as on many international race tracks, "amber" is understood to signify "start your motors"), or that a streetside stand no longer exists due to a driver's need to adjust a dashboard music player. Such tragedies could have been prevented if this city's drivers had simply stopped, looked, and listened.

In fairness, I, too, am a vehicular operator. I, too, have been guilty of "minor infractions," and I, too, have used the excuse that "everyone else drives that way" to "cover" my transgressions. Sometimes, following the crowd in speed or in tenacity keeps me and my passengers safe (especially when the drivers behind me are mere centimeters from my fender and we are traveling on a major byway). Other times, though, in fairness, my behavior is hypocritical at best, dangerous to other roadsters and to walkers at worst (especially when I gamble on how long a light will remain green or when I pass another car in a popular, but ethically questionable, manner).

The solution to my and to other Israeli drivers' lack of sensibility is mindfulness. Additional means of enforcing driving laws need not be enacted (such a change, even if it saved only one life, would be invaluable). Rather, at the level of the street, drivers must work to constantly remember that others also use the road.

Jerusalem is a holy and beautiful city. It's a pity to mar such exquisiteness by having to fear for our lives.

— Hannah

A Difficult Confluence of Events

My Adar felt topsy-turvy. On the one side, a contemporary hero of mine revealed a hurt, which that person and that person's family had received at the hands of other Jews. On the other side, I experienced my own hurt when a Jew treated me with *condescension.*

Neither my hero nor I like getting dissed. Both of us hold our resources as being as valuable as are those of other members of the worldwide Jewish community. Neither of us wants to be: interrupted, kept apart from, or otherwise transformed into an object of verbal or physical projectiles.

All Jews are equally valuable. Even so, Jews are imperfect. Whereas I was horribly disappointed to hear hurt become what sounded like hate in my hero's mouth, and whereas I was thunderstruck when a Jewish leader did violence to me, I know my personality flaws are likely more glaring than are those of the people who attacked either of us. I have to think this way.

Fortunately, my Adar also included a wedding. The guests at that joyous occasion were an eclectic group ranging from the forward-looking fellow with gelled, spiked hair to the traditional rabbi dressed in black and white. Some of the female guests came in jeans. Other female attendees wore outfits that covered all but their hands and faces. The two honored families greeted each well-wisher with equal warmth.

I cleave to the beliefs that The Infinite loves each and every one of us and that we are bid to emulate that behavior of The Boss. It is not for me to cast aspersions on other Jews, publicly or in the secret places of my heart, that is, it is not for me to loathe them because they think, act, or offer up opinions antithetical to my own, or because they hurt me. Whereas I called someone outside of Israel with the intention of discussing the ill treatment I had received from the callous Jew, I never did broach that topic with my friend. In the end, I am glad to report, I could not bring myself to issue sour words about another member of our tribe. Instead, my friend and I spoke of her forthcoming immigration to Israel.

At the wedding, the food was delicious. The groom and bride's friends employed many fantastic gimmicks to entertain the new couple. The bridal party and the groom's family looked regal. Nonetheless, the most outstanding quality of that night was the way in which the hosts mingled naturally with all of their guests. Their celebration was exceptional in its ability to cohesively and concurrently pull all of its participants to a higher level of consciousness. When I, for example, offered my "mazel tov" to the bride's grandmother, a woman dressed in a *sheitel*, a wig, (I wore a scarf), I saw that this matriarch was surrounded by girls in pants and by girls in skirts, and that she was authentically issuing love to each and every young lady.

Her actions not only taught mighty lessons to her generations, but they also provided us revelers with a corner of heaven. The Almighty does send us guides to prepare us for *Moshiach*, the Messiah. We just have to look.

My hero has new and exciting projects to actualize. At the same time, that Jew's existent body of work is easy to admire. I just wish pain hadn't so palpably permeated that Jew's communication. Since we have common professional interests, for personal reasons, as well, I hope that he can get past the emotional trauma. I'm praying to The Holy One, Blessed be He, to replace bitterness with joy.

As per the Jew who assailed me, we, too, have handfuls of people in common. Despite the fact that I cried for hours after the incident, telling my family, without identifying the aggressor, that no one, including their wife and mom, ought to be degraded to the status of a nonentity, the best that I can do, in that case, is to adjust my expectations. I cannot hate that person, but I likely will, for a time, continue to loathe their choices. I can't adjudicate their behavior. I can pray. Torah speaks chapters about deep, cosmic loneliness. I hope that the Jew in question quickly finds both meaning and sagacious company.

The wedding was so much more *heimishe*, home-like, than are most that I wanted to sit and to talk, to share and to listen, to stretch out that experience, to savor it with my friends. To wit, Computer Cowboy and I lingered longer than we had at many similar events. There is something wonderful in the simple goodness constituted by inclusion. There is something mind-blowing in witnessing acceptance that has no bounds. I'm convinced that at that wedding canopy, where all Jews were welcomed, the cherubim of the Holy Ark readily faced each other.

From Under a Rock

I guess I've been living with a little more insularity than I realized. Only, literally, yesterday did I hear about the horrific goings-on in Nachlaot.

I'm not a psychologist. I'm not a corrections officer. I'm simply a mom who is also a "word person" and who was once a professor of the social sciences. If the little bit I can do to help secure and save our children is to make sure that the topic of child abuse stays current, then I'm glad to be putting in my two shekels' worth. If, in turn, each of us did our little bit, per se, more kids would be safer; fewer molesters would cause shocking crimes, and larger numbers of victims would be able to journey more easily toward surviving their ordeals, that is to say, larger numbers of victims would be able to journey toward wholeness.

Meanwhile, I'm struck. I hurt. I hurt for the parents. I hurt for the kids. I hurt, especially for the kids, who, G-d forbid, will not get adequate or sufficiently long-term treatment. I hurt for the future victims of those unresolved victims, regardless of whether those future victims are assaulted, exposed, or are otherwise made to suffer when those unresolved victims are still children, or later, when those unresolved victims have aged into adults.

Whereas not all victims remain unresolved, and whereas not all unresolved victims become, in turn, abusers, if only 10% of unresolved victims become offenders, with each successive generation, more and more innocent souls will get fractured. Stopping abuse is not merely about catching current perpetrators and about healing current, known victims; stopping abuse is necessarily also about finding "hidden" victims and about preventing them from continuing the cycle. Such a complete response to this vileness is necessary.

As Paul E. Mullen and Jillian Fleming explain in "Long-Term Effects of Child Sexual Abuse," a publication of the Australian Government's National Child Protection Clearinghouse, "the fundamental damage inflicted by child sexual abuse is to the child's developing capacities for trust, intimacy, agency and sexuality."[25] In other words, the pain of sexual abuse often lasts a lifetime and often impacts survivors in deeply profound ways.

Their relationships to themselves, their relationships to their intimates, their relationships to their acquaintances, and their relationships to strangers, all are, often, severely marred.

Why is this form of hurt so bad? Helpguide.org., an American source for information about professional information on mental and emotional health, edited by Jeanne and Robert Segal, posits, in "Recognizing and Preventing Child Abuse," that "child sexual abuse is an especially complicated form of abuse because of its layers of guilt and shame."[26]

One of the issues concomitant to this type of grievous suffering is that even when this type of abuse has been acknowledged by powerful others, i.e., by the adults in a child's world, thereafter, this type of abuse might get rationalized, minimized, or completely denied by those same authorities.

Blaming the victim, a far too common form of rationalization, for example, adds to the trauma that a child victim experiences, as does making light of what that victim reports. Given that, as the Segals report, "sexual abuse doesn't always involve body contact,"[27] adults escape their responsibility to protect children via the many cultural loopholes available to adults.

Back to the Segals, we see that "exposing a child to sexual situations or material is sexually abusive, whether or not touching is involved."[28] In the Nachlaot situation, unfortunately, some of the children were forced to watch others children being tortured. It is possible that the children made to witness such atrocities will be more deeply wounded that those upon whom the acts were perpetrated. If adults, who are trained to deal with wide varieties of crises, need help after witnessing child abuse, then children—people who are, by definition, vulnerable—will need help processing their experiences that much more so. Yet, that group of kids has been rubriced, by some people, as "mere" witnesses. Any children or adult impacted by such deeds suffers deeply.

Last, in terms of empowered persons making little of such crimes against the weakest members of humanity, many folk fall back into the false comforts offered by repudiation. Grownups sometimes unwittingly befriend a child abuser. Other times, grownups intentionally deny the events that they earlier had acknowledged. Sexual abuse of children is scary stuff. Period. People have a tendency to run away when they are afraid.

Sadly, such retractions worsen the harm done to victimized children. Psychotherapist David L. Calof, as quoted in McClendon, explains that children whose ghastly experiences are invalidated have trouble with

186

identity as well as with social rules and norms.[29] It's bad enough when the powerful people in a child's life, such as that child's neighbors, religious leaders, doctors, police, parents, or other adults hurt them. It's worse when additional authoritative people tell that same child to forget about the dark incidents he or she endured. No one needs a university degree to grasp why such a double dose of betrayal cripples souls.

Furthermore, pedophiles didn't discern among secular, Dati or Charadei children; they hurt all of them. Nachlaot, for instance, is a mixed community. The victims in that neighborhood came from the entire array of its population.

Just as this problem breaks children from every type of home, the response needs to come from all of us. Not only can we help prevent further such incidents, but as Jews, we are obliged to act. To turn away from such unpleasantries is the equivalent of shirking our responsibility for *pikuach nefesh, for* saving a life.

Solutions will involve lots of steps, by lots of people. They will also require a large investment of time.

As aforementioned, I have no easy answers. I write about such unimaginable badness to keep the point in the forefront of our thinking. All of us people who care about children need to act on this matter. As we progress, all of us will benefit from raising our awareness regarding child safety.

Embracing Alternatives

I make no pretense that my wisdoms are anything but earned. My innate qualities do not include the tendency to stay, unaided, on a particular route. More so, any merit I've gleaned has, mercifully, been gifted to me by The Greater Sagacity. Any proclivity of mine to correct my drift comes from The One and Only Source.

Accordingly, when I'm less than clear-headed, when it seems to me that important ideas to which I've been exposed manage to pull me toward sensible conclusions, I make efforts to take into account that my process is not natural, but is otherworldly directed. Analogously, I work to remember that my parenting—those acts in which I, as a mother, allegedly engage in to support and to encourage my offspring—gets significantly assisted.

Despite the fact that a dear one, among my brood, is successfully growing within the framework of an alternative school, it took me many painful years to embrace the Torah sentiment, which I had often espoused but had not lived, that each child ought to be educated according to his or her needs. When it came to actualizing that concept, I fell to the demons of "what if."

I lost my compass to: "what if my family, who is already known as speaking a range of levels of Hebrew (the kids are fluent; their parents are not), and who is already known to consist, entirely, of *Baali Teshuva,* of people who have "returned" to G-d, gets further stigmatized," "what if the beloved in question never learns rudimentary Torah concepts" (the school, a Sudbury institution, focuses on social and psychological well-being and leaves choices about the content and the mode of learning up to each child), and "what if, by sending my offspring there, instead of spending additional years trying to force that little one into the mold into which that little one clearly does not fit, I cause that child to be mucked up forever and ever?" In brief, I forgot Who maneuvers life's bus.

Whereas the rhetoric: of appreciating the good in humanity, of needing to cultivate the inner wealth of individuals, and of stepping away from casting judgments comes easily to me, the implementation of the same does not. Sure, failing to remove myself from witnessing and from deciding another being's worth is silly as well as is wrought with troubles, and, sure, failing to disregard other folks' witnessing and deciding my family members' worth is equally silly and equally wrought with troubles. However, pretending to be powerful, or pretending that I can coast on others' opinions, lets me, delusionally, and temporarily, delay coping with difficulties.

In short, failing to bank on The Name's will messes with my otherwise fundamentally good experiences. From the moment I pretend that I run the cosmic transportation company, or from the moment that I begin to believe that I ought to yield my powers, illusionary or real, to others' whims, I am skunked. Not only does my faith start to shake, but my entire self drops into deep, dark places, too.

I don't like deep, dark places.

I also don't like challenges. I don't like the ones that I can't comprehend, and I don't like the ones that I can comprehend. I never asked to have one of my children become traumatized from the absorption process and, concurrently, to regard the "regular" system of religious schooling as more than barbed. In balance, I have not been and will not be given the steering wheel.

So, my kid attends a nontraditional school. Bless G-d, in the first year, alone, a lot of healing took place. School became, once more, a location of safety. Teachers became, once more, beneficent. Classmates became, once more, friends and learning partners.

This year, my child's second year at the alternative school, is a time of other sorts of growth, in a good eye. In Sudbury schools, children are free to stretch as far and as fast as they are willing and able. In such places, children integrate subjects and children come to regard basics as the tools with which they will function in the adult world. For instance, a child, in this sort of school, might learn higher math, but not because of an impending SAT or *bagrut,* matriculation exam; rather, that child reaches to learn because he or she wants that knowledge in order to pursue physics or engineering.

Similarly, in such a school, cooking can be a jumping-off point for learning about economics, chemistry, and interpersonal communication, and the raising of small animals can provide an impetus for learning about ecology, biology, and law. The pursuit of a theatre experience might, in such an environment, similarly catalyze a student to learn about playwriting, about small business management, about stage craft, and about public speaking.

In truth, the possibilities inherent in a Sudbury education are boundless. If only worried parents, like me, could learn to release our imagined control, we would enjoy our sons' and daughters' growth, that much more.

I do not know how and when my child will catch up on his religious education. That domain, as is true of other areas of expertise in his new school, is open for students to explore at a personal pace. Whereas Jerusalem, Bless G-d, has a plethora of well-credentialed Torah teachers, many of whom would be happy to be hired for tutoring, this aspect of my child's life, too, must be student-centric.

What I do know is that day by day, week by week, year by painful year, my child is becoming reacquainted with his innate potential. My child is integrating the concept of self-worth.

Less importantly, my dear one is starting to learn about many topics at a self-driven speed. Recent "news" from that kid includes, but is not limited to: talk of nuclear propulsion, research on agriculture, on robotics, and on team building, and some grousing about the role of variables, of fractions, and of the like in the aforementioned projects.

I see a trickle-down effect, as well. In familial relations, that child is taking a larger role. That little one is actively seeking to participate in the governance of the family and has become comfortable objecting to certain parent-generated rules and to certain sibling interactions.

Fortunately, that sweet soul has years of primary and of secondary education left. Hopefully, The Boss, Who planted that precious soul in my body, Who governed that sweet one's birth, and Who has never left that child (or any of the rest of us, for that matter) to quake alone, will continue to give that beloved the exact measure of fulfillment required for that beloved's needs. When I remember Who is in control, I anticipate a happy ending.

I've never, truly, regarded myself as "alternative," but merely as mindful in my parenting, yet I've come to grasp that there are additional degrees of "openness" to which I can ready myself. As usual, my children are my teachers.

Taking an unconventional route is not only called for in select cases, be that route home schooling (which, for example, succeeded extremely well for a friend, whose older son is in his third (!) year at prestigious, post-secondary yeshiva), be that route enrolling a child in a nontraditional school (as is the case, today, in my family), or be that route enrolling a child in a secular institution (with which others of my friends have had the best results for their sons and daughters), but is, also, for some precious children of Torah Jews, the only correct answer. Parental trust comes in the form of knowing that we must walk the path that The Holy One, Blessed be He, designated for each of our families.

Student Loans and Other Absorption Fantasies

When I pursued my education in the New World, like the majority of my peers, I took out student loans from the federal government. In those days, student loans were annually renewable, temporary allotments of money, available at interest levels that were significantly subsidized by the nation's common legislating body. Most young folk pursuing higher education took advantage of those programs.

For the majority of us debtors, as well as for the United States Government, the program was a win-win situation. Upon graduating and joining the work force, we paid back our obligations. Meanwhile, our nation, still smarting from its loss of face in the international space race (and later in the science and math race), benefited from a new generation of trained professionals.

Theoretically, acculturating to life in Israel can be compared to taking out those student loans. Initially, like those collegiate borrowers, new immigrants are beholden; we "owe" a debt to more socially integrated individuals and to social institutions that help us with our absorption process. Not too long thereafter, when we are more or less autonomous, we "pay back" our obligations by providing help to other, newer citizens.

For the majority of us newcomers, as well as for the social fabric into which we are integrating, this informal "program" is a win-win situation. Upon gaining our "sea legs," and joining the work force, we become "givers" rather than "takers." Meanwhile, our society, which in some ways is still smarting from the lopsidedness of certain immigration floods, benefits from its new harvest of trained professionals.

In real life, the above types of programs are not fail-safe. Individuals default on loans. Immigrants sink into severe financial, psychological, or other types of problems, or even elect, in tiny numbers, to return to the climes from which they came.

What's interesting to me is why these systemic failures occur. Whereas I am no longer directly invested, literally or figuratively, in the American student loan programs, I am very much invested, both literally and figuratively, in immigration to Israel.

First, not all mentors are equally perspicacious. Not only is graduate school, in part, about professional networking, but so, too, is immigration into Israel. A savvy professor can help an emerging scholar land a first job and, perhaps, even help him or her find an editor amenable to publishing his or her first piece of research. Similarly, a savvy friend, relative, or agency director can help an emerging immigrant land a first job here, or can otherwise help him or her get noticed for future career opportunities. Unfortunately, sagacity does not seem to be evenly distributed. Sometimes, the college kid who attached him or herself to an academic with scruples is rewarded for such appropriate behavior by being shunned at conferences and in organizational circles.

Sometimes, well-intended immigrants miss out on employment because they've stuck to principles that are not as commonplace as they could be in Israel. Whereas the "good guy" does, in fact, usually "win," the eventuality that spans the "good guy's" first efforts and his final results can be long and difficult.

Second, not all comers have equivalent personal resources. In graduate school, some students are more gifted than others. Some students have better study habits than others. Some kiss up. Some play frightening (to me) games with faculty in order to get ahead. I recall a fellow who was doing the grunt work on a workbook, which accompanied a freshman level text. He was our hero… until we, his classmates, found out that he was using over-the-counter drugs to compensate for the sleep he was missing in order to perform that unpaid, mind-numbing labor. Also, most of us knew of at least a few persons who slept their way through school (in this second case, the "lie-down" has little to do with slumber).

Analogously, whereas I know hard working immigrants, immigrants who trust implicitly in The Name, I also know persons who think cheating the government, cheating their employers, cheating their colleagues, or cheating the general public is okay if such corruption secures their future. Those individuals have no qualms with multiple sets of books or of prices. Those individuals have no problem pushing, literally, to the head of a line. Those individuals justify their use of dishonesty in speech as a means to find a place for themselves and their families in society.

Third, not all graduate students or immigrants arrive at their new destinies with similar expectations. Though many are idealistic, some come jaded and are otherwise prejudiced against the system into which they hope to become incorporated. Those students, who see school as a means to an end as opposed to an end in itself, that is, as opposed to a special prospect, perform differently in class and act differently at professional gatherings than do the students who are more forthrightly minded. The former "perform" their roles, but are unfriendly and competitive. The latter work with their peers together to accomplish goals and remain gracious.

In Israeli society, the aforementioned divisive behavior manifests itself in a variety of experiences, including in: gender-related armed services appointments, bickering that occurs over religious authority, and a multi-tiered salary system. Some of us, unfortunately, have even stopped questioning why there exists such a large gulf between the "haves" and the "have nots," here. Too often, an individual in an aisle seat refuses to yield to the grandfather aiding an elderly wife. Too often, cars nearly run down small children. Too often, we walk past the fellow Jew who has an outstretched arm.

Fortunately, our society is home to compassionate members, as well. Mothers watch each other's children. Organizations supply *kallot*, brides, with basic needs. Grocery bills are paid, anonymously, for each other.

Fourth, not all graduate students or all immigrants arrive at their new destinies with equivalent familial or financial support. Some students (and immigrants) receive regular emails, phone calls, or other types of encouragements. Some do not. Some students (and immigrants) easily shed the influence of materialism upon their climbing of levels. Some do not.

One graduate student that I knew drove a car and owned a townhouse. Another traveled first class to visit his parents' home when he had a break between semesters. A third sent all of her clothing to the dry cleaners. The rest of us had communal pasta dinners, loaned each other typewriter ribbons when the stationary stores were closed, and carried parcels to various points for each other.

Similarly, in Israel, there are citizens who announce their job titles and European vacation plans before asking if a newcomer needs help finding his or her way in a neighborhood. There are persons who forget the widow and the orphan, and then audaciously complain, aloud, that such individuals contribute less to community coffers than do other folks. There are even denizens who create payment ceilings over which their peers necessarily stumble. Yet, there are, likewise, outsized families, who regularly manage to put yet another chair at their table, and who manage to cut a single chicken

194

into even smaller bits. There are children who remember to pass only nice clothes to area *gemachim*, free loan societies. There are leaders who march ahead of their troops, rather than stay behind in safety and comfort.

In Israel, as in post-secondary education, among mentors, attitudes and actual physical resources differ. Most of these disparities can be overcome or compensated for. Most immigrants do not "default" on their loans, appreciating that their access to Israel's holiness is inestimable. Most newbies remain part of this system, eagerly anticipating the time when they, in turn, can aid other immigrants.

I'm Okay, You're Okay, but Bring OU

I confess that I guffawed when Missy Younger relayed to me that her friends, all of whom are native-born Israelis, regard KOF-K, a *hecsher*, a kashrut mark, that is near and dear to my New World family, as "exotic." In the Old World, KOF-K, and a handful of additional kashrut symbols, such as "OU," such as "OK," and such as "Star K," is fairly universally accepted. While yet other certifications, as exemplified by "cRc," by "COR," and by "the *Bais Din of Crown Heights*," too, are well esteemed at New World tables, where careful adherence to kashrut laws takes place, these symbols do not seem to be, on the whole, globally as well-known as they are in North America.

Analogously, when my family made immigration to Israel, before we had a chance to acquire a LOR, a Local Orthodox Rabbi, we relied on the advice of a well-informed friend, who had earned ordination, and who was learning at a renowned *kollel*, at an institute for full-time, advanced study of the Talmud and rabbinic literature, to guide us on which symbols we ought to trust in this Old World. He suggested: "Badatz Agudat Yisrael," "Badatz Eida Chareidis," "Rav Rubin," and "Badatz Rav Yaakov Landau." Later, we learned about: "Belz" ("Machzikei Hadas"), "Chug Chatam Sofer," and "Shearit Yisrael."

Kashrut is a beautiful category of mitzvot, yet kashrut can make a proficient homemaker crazy, even during non-*shmittah* years, even during years when the land is not left to lie fallow and when all agricultural activity, including plowing, planting, pruning, and harvesting, is not forbidden by The Law. One of the first questions we officially asked our local rabbi, once we acquired a local rabbi, concerned what to do about eating at a home or at a celebration of another Jew, who might accept different symbols than do we (our friends, Bless G-d, are even more heterogeneous here than they were in the New World). Our rabbi's answer (don't try this at home folks; one cannot rely on the answer formally given to another Jew) was that if the woman of the house covers her hair, is *shomer mitzvot*, observant of mitzvot (including, but not limited to Sabbath observant), and is *shomer kashrut*, observant of the laws of kashrut, we could accept her food or the food of her designated agent, e.g. her caterer. What's more, we were admonished that kashrut is meant, in part, to unify Jews, and that we ought not to enter into the fray, birthed from fear, of not holding to sufficient numbers of fences.

Since I am neither learned nor interested in feeding conflict, I will suggest that certain specifics of kashrut are personal: to individuals, to families, to communities, and so forth, and that kashrut decisions must be made in a predictable and consistent manner as supervised by a rabbi. My family keeps more stringencies than do some members of our community so that members of other communities, who are sometimes our guests, and who lean toward many stringencies, can feel fully comfortable in our home.

Meanwhile, there remains the issue of knowing whether or not it's acceptable to eat at various businesses. Until very recently, the website *Jerusalem Kosher News* was a wonderful font of information about who was holding by which symbols. Regardless, eating out remains a "buyer beware" situation; check the kashrut certification, and do not rely on the word of employees or on signage painting on a façade or elsewhere, as to who is certifying a restaurant's, a grocery store's, or a caterer's kashrut.

Accordingly, it's not a bad idea to make ourselves useful to tourists or to others who happen to be temporarily in the Holy Land. As Rabbi Hillel evoked, "what is hateful to you, do not do to another." I think most of us would be miffed, in the least, if we were strangers in a realm and ate something we regretted, or if we missed something we desired because no one helped us navigate the local certification system.

Finally, at the same time as my children's friends, and some of Computer Cowboy's and my friends, remain as weary of New World symbols as they do of *Ashkenazi*, Eastern European Jewry's, delights, like gefilte fish, or of Yemenite treats, such as *schug*, hot sauce, depending on their backgrounds, it is likewise the case that they will eat around items made with OU or with other New World-certified ingredients when they are joining us at our table. We accommodate our dear ones as much as is reasonable, but try not to drive ourselves crazy.

Sigh. Just when I was getting comfortable with separating meat from milk, with carefully checking my lentils, fruits, and vegetables, and with making sure that my cakes tasted good (not an issue of kashrut, but an issue of hospitality), I had to return to rethinking which kashrut marks, among the ones used by my family, would make our guests most comfortable.

Oh well; merit is given according to difficulty. In the interim, I contend that I'm okay, you're okay, and to my home, even if you don't grasp this mark's authentic goodness, please feel free to bring OU.

Neither Location nor Worldview

As we count up toward Shavuot, we are reminded that the entire community of the Jews received the Torah. Let's look at what we become empowered to do when we get over ourselves, when we stop focusing on judging others, and when we start concentrating on self-improvement.

Recently, a pal and I were discussing what's attractive in people. We agreed that we are drawn to character traits. Granted, friends with fiduciary means are able, if motivated, to pay our way at coffee time. Granted, friends endowed with muscles can help us get our packages onto buses. Granted, friends who are whiz kids are able to aid us in mental crunches. Yet, money, strength, and intelligence are fleeting. Whereas those qualities are necessary, they are far from sufficient for good living. More important is an overarching yearning to correct our individual paths in order to better our internal worlds.

Happily, the holy route of self-betterment is not indigenous to location or to worldview. Rather, it is dependent on what we think, on what we say, and on how we act. Searching for means to link to The Boss, guarding our mouths from evil, specifically from derogatory speech, and engaging in deeds of loving kindness, all are means to developing ourselves.

What's more, these tracks for self-growth, especially the particulars of: truth, proper use of time, diligence, honor, serenity, gentleness, cleanliness, patience, order, humility, righteousness, frugality, and guarding one's tongue, can be embraced whether we live in North America, in Europe, in South Africa, in the Middle East, or elsewhere. Also, these deeds are not dependent upon our perspective, that is, upon the nature of our religious ideology.

In all of the social worlds in which I've merited to live, proper conduct has been valued. It is just as important to my American secular circle of associates, as it is to my American religious circle of associates, as it is to my Israeli religious circle of associates that we have matzah on Passover, that we prayfor children stricken with cancer, that we make an effort to speak authentic, good words about each other, that we avoid gossip, and that we have a spiritual bridge, a connection to *Shamayim*, Heaven.

The differences in the ways in which we perform acts of loving kindness need not be awkward. Diversity has a place within the context of Torah's rules. There's room for us to applaud our peers who bless their children, without us getting caught up in whether our peers appoint the same adults, during the same occasions, to sanctify those younger heads, as we do to sanctify our families' young heads. Likewise, it's okay, maybe even meritorious, circumstances depending, if our friends and relatives use different kashrut symbols than we do. Perhaps they are more stringent. Perhaps they are less so, but are more meritorious in the degree to which they have extended themselves in order to practice the stricture.

Taking it upon ourselves to measure our dear ones' worth, G-d forbid, no matter the topic, is ill-suited to our aspiring to greater and greater levels of devotion. More exactly, we ought to focus on building up our own souls and on building them up one small bit at a time.

Whether or not we Jews are blessed to live in Jerusalem, blessed to be able to devote the majority of our time to learning Torah, or blessed to know how to take joy from the mundanities that make up our days and nights, is, at some point, moot. To espouse the opposite is problematic, is a position that implies that only a highly limited number of ways of existing count at all as good. Instead, let's, no matter where we stand, literally or figuratively, hold our own selves accountable for our mentations, words, and behaviors.

It remains of no benefit to us to claim that we are stuck because we have lost our motivation to work on ourselves, or to claim that we are stuck by dint of our geography or by dint of our religious practice. Ascension has, does, and will continue to rely on our acceptance of our starting points, coupled with our willingness to move forward from those places. Neither our location nor our worldview, ultimately, can impede us if we reach for personal betterment. We ought not to waste our resources disparaging ourselves, accordingly. We ought not to cry for opportunities we perceive as missed because of our *topoi*.

Blaring among the Mustards

Judaism is an identity. Israel is the Jewish home. Jews can no more divorce themselves from Israel than they can wittingly pluck their souls from their bodies. Passion necessarily follows these axioms.

I'm blaring among the mustards. The melodies of Udi Davidi, a folk singer who brings to life *Psalms*, is pouring out of my stereo. I have cranked the sound up so high that if I let my left hand linger on my car door, as the dust of the outside world blows past, I can feel my speakers' vibrations. What's more, people outside of my car, too, can hear my patriotic music.

I am home. This is my home. This land has always and will always be home for me and for my people.

Accordingly, as I travel among hostile spots, I keep my windows rolled down. My songs proclaim pride in ownership.

This land was my forefather's. It is mine. It is my children's heritage.

Ordinarily, I am quiet. I own no television, seek out no movies, and disdain loud compositions, both in my apartment, and, as can be heard through the walls, in the apartments of my neighbors. I reflexively shudder when passing by buildings spilling over with shattering thuds and insist that my children, adolescents to a one, muffle their tunes with headphones or similar devices. I am not the queen of extraneous reverberations.

Nonetheless, I have no remorse for either the tears that streak my cheeks or for the decibels that escape my automobile as I drive along my native soil. If I had a license, perhaps I'd as well be shooting a gun into the sky. My declaration is consequential.

You see, our checkpoints have been vacated. Our civil government has pulled our soldiers away from the peripheries over which they used to watch. Meanwhile, our emboldened cousins run crazy through our countryside. When I drive to a nearby village for a circumcision's festive meal or for a wedding, I now do so without human aid; only Heaven any longer protects me.

Travel through the chambers of my motherland has ceased to be a route of certainty.

Each time, before I drive, I pray for safe passage and for safe return. Yet, my cousins transport without restraint, fearing no harm, knowing that the world's media is their purchased watchdog.

In the universities where I teach, those cousins fill seats. They recuperate in my hospitals. They take jobs in my corporate centers. They make a ruckus in order to use my roads unencumbered, to receive humanitarian aid from my people, specifically, and to ratchet up the nature of the handouts, of which they take delivery, from all of humanity, in general.

At the same time, my kin, who do not hurt outsiders because of temporary corporeal or cerebral indigestion, who do not set children ablaze with bombs because it's easy and impersonal, and who do not force young women to choose between rape and suicide, because of compromised mores, would never dare to enter my cousins' social institutions. No amount of linguistic prowess or even of firearm power could guarantee my kind any sort of sanctuary among those others.

The funny thing is that despite the fact that their leadership skims the best of their resources and catalyzes the destruction of our reservoirs, those others lead the planet in clamoring for my people's demise. The prophets foresaw such an exigency. I live it.

So, on this temperate morning, during this span when I am not free to enter and to exist, let alone to linger, in domains that are part of my homeland, I turn up the volume. In the same way as the mustards blossom, the milk thistles salute with speckled leaves, the cyclamens open toward the sky, and the wee blue and green grasses sprout, I mean to scream to anyone who might hear me.

I am all but tepid in my intentionality. I am of this nation. This nation is mine.

Something Meaningful in the Violence Here

Minutes after I leave my home, I pull over to the shoulder of the road. I pull over in a "friendly" community; my drive transverses all sorts of neighborhoods.

At the curb, I recite *"Tefilat HaDerech,"* "The Travelers' Prayer." Whereas I am grateful to have a temporary teaching job, I am wary of my employment's location; a Jewish city in the region known as "Samaria." Although, at least at the time of this writing, that area is protected by the state's military, and although that area contains friendly communities, I feel uneasy when driving to, from, and within that realm.

In counterpoint, I know many people who think my family is nuts for living in such a "dangerous" place as Jerusalem, let alone living anywhere in this entire spiritual, though "dangerous" nation. Those individuals prefer to trust in straw or in wood, rather than in the stone of the commandment of settling this land.

Likewise, I am blessed to know many Israelis who see life from the opposite perspective. This second group of friends thinks my family is nuts for not insisting on the right to drive throughout our homeland, for not encouraging more people to become scholar-warriors, etc. These people think I am crazy for not taking the shortest route to work, and for, instead, taking the "safest" one.

I lack answers. On the one hand, my immediate family embraced the opportunity to live in the world's holiest city. On the other hand, the path I take to work takes almost twice as long as does the "short" path. Further, given the risks associated with traveling in the region where my college is located, I felt a need to ask for guidance before accepting my job (the answer I received was to take the assignment).

In spite of that religious directive, I remain unnerved. On my route to work, I pass not only our communities, but also the settlements of our Biblical cousins. Whereas the majority of license plates I spot are ours, others, amazingly, are theirs.

As for my students, they are: religious Jews and secular Jews, Russian Jews, Ethiopian Jews, Yemenite Jews, and locals. They are also Muslim Arabs and Christian Arabs. Some students carry visible guns. Some sit and stand as though they carry hidden weapons. During recess, we talk about martial arts and about the many possible ways of killing a person.

When each meeting of my classes ends, I am grateful to chauffeur students back to Jerusalem, gratis. I do not want to drive the area's roads, checkpoints notwithstanding, alone, in the dark. And yet, reading with my class about the insanity in other places leads me to appreciate that there is something meaningful in the violence here.

Specifically, one piece, which my class and I prepared in our efforts to better my students' comprehension of English, was an article about the perpetuation of violence in North America and in Europe, as social violence is catalyzed by the technological components of those cultures. More specifically, that essay referred to the ways in which: the violent content of the media, especially of television and of movies, the violent content of the Internet, and the violent content of video games, together, modify social norms. That is, popular pastimes in "civilized" countries increase social tolerance for mindless aggression. Cultural numbing to mindless aggression, in turn, increases the social appetite for depictions of, and for engagements in, violence, and so forth, until violent products and services insidiously become part of the social fiber.

Profiteers, i.e., individuals more interested in acquiring material wealth than in obtaining spiritual solvency, respond to this cycling social appetite by creating and distributing progressively more violent products. Eventually, such goods are sold and are distributed not only in answer to "general" demand, but also in anticipation of identifiable, and often warped, demographic and psycho-graphic market niches.

That means that over time, the meaning of social "normalcy" changes until society considers it blasé to react to even school children's carnage. For example, music videos, in "modern" countries, sample graphic clips from news stations' pictorial accounts of murders. They show children riding their pedal-powered bikes to execute their enemies. They show youths as having no compunction about shooting-up entire classrooms full of innocent peers.

In my Old World college classroom, my weapon-bearing, often highly-spirited students looked at me with greater and greater interest as we got deeper and deeper into that reading. They know that I am a product of the

New World, of a place where mass media, Internet, and video games are seemingly as cheap as bubble gum. They know that I am also a product of a religious environment, of a place where life is the most precious of all commodities, and where saving a life ranks among the highest of deeds.

It was palpable that my students were bewildered about how the middle-aged mama, who had spent weeks professing to them explicitly about English, and implicitly about good character, would resolve the paradox. "Hypocrisy" does not bode well in the Middle East. My students became very quiet. I, too, was stilled.

In light of some of the grander trends in the world, which my students and I had just publicly deconstructed, I was finding it increasingly difficult to maintain my stance of intolerance. Perhaps, there is a difference between intentionality and heedlessness, when it comes to violent solutions to critical problems. Perhaps not. Regardless of which side of the regional conflict my college students and their respective people support, their killings are more often than not about beliefs. Their killings are more often than not purposeful acts of violence. Their killings are more often than not extremely meaningful.

Perhaps, there is no difference between premeditated murder and unlawful killings that lack malice. It is wrong to inflict grievous harm or death. My faith very clearly articulates the necessity of yielding even the most sacred limits to protect life. My faith puts many strictures around depriving anyone of their existence. That evening, in my college classroom, deep in the middle of hostile territory, which in turn sits deep in the middle of my motherland, an allegedly "mundane" essay, which I was reviewing with my students for the purposes of expanding their command of English grammar and vocabulary caused me to better appreciate life.

It is still my intention to pull over to the curb and to pray every time I leave Jerusalem. The only true shield from danger is the covering provided by G-d. It is still my plan to toss dangerous students out of my classroom, and to check the shrubbery near my car, as well as to check my back seat, before I drive home. We partner with G-d in our personal security. And yet, when I pull over, when I shut the car door, and when I check my immediate environment, I now do so in a context that is anything but arbitrary.

Moving Forward

I find myself yet a bit fiddly concerning the nonchalance with which the average person, here, in Israel, is responding to international politics. Albeit, I am no lover of the *sturm und drang*, storm and stress, which envelopes most global goings-on, I am disappointed, in the least, that folks have settled down, seemingly, to matters of: local soccer, national elections, and Chanukah *gelt*, monetary gifts.

Whereas there's little that is moral or even fair, at a intellectual level, about bullies coveting our land and about their trying to attain it by insidious means ('cause they can't win in a fair "altercation" of brain or of brawn), it disappoints me that we, as a nation, are not responding with more fervor to these goings-on. Sure, *Moshiach*, the Messiah, is promised to arrive when all of the lands unite against Israel, but I'd think a little fervor, on our part, is in order.

Passion is appropriate when tyrants are given a long leash. It was this Holy Land, after all, in a recent military conflagration, which controlled her fire when being pummeled by vast numbers of propelled enemy weapons. It was this Holy Land, after all, which struck surgically at the opposition, rather than throwing her missiles into the air, per se, heedless of where they might come down, as would have been justified by the other side's actions. It is this Holy Land, after all, which continues to send humanitarian aid to her enemies and to admit them to her hospitals because we, the Jews of Israel, put life before just about anything else.

Sadly, it is this Holy Land, after all, which is hunched over and is nearly playing dead. Except for the rationale of profits, or for dreams of future profits (logical, but evil, as an end to which to aspire), I don't get the gist of our "leaders'" motivation. Even if those politicos are selfish to a point of fiduciary exclusion, don't they want to survive? Don't they care about their families and their friends? Don't they want to enjoy children and grandchildren?

Color me naïve, but I had assumed that even the most self-serving of individuals wanted more than to be king of this island for a fleeting span. Breathing is so underrated.

Meanwhile, Hassan Nasrallah and his cronies can stomp their collective feet, wave their sabers and make much noise from here to eternity (which, itself, might occur sooner than later given Iran's arsenal). Most homespun Israelis could not care less. The UN can pass resolution after resolution. Most homespun Israelis could not care less. We denizens of this sacred realm are waiting for a catalyst. We are willing to act.

In this season, in the weekly Torah portion, "*Veyeishev*," we contemplate Yoseph's successful solution, specifically (albeit after a very long time in jail), to his trouble with the wife of Potiphar, the wife of an important Egyptian official. We learn of Yoseph's refusal, in general, to divest his faith. No matter how high up the foreign food chain that Yaakov's son climbed, including to the height of viceroy, Yoseph held fast to the essence of Judaism.

What's more, in this season of Chanukah, we read of Yehudite's successful confrontation with Holofernes, a mighty Syrian-Greek general, and we study the deeds of Hannah, who rallied the Jews against the barbaric Greek requirement that Jewish maidens sleep first with outlander officials and, only thereafter, with their husbands.

Yehudite, daughter of Yochanan the high priest, murdered her advisory without automated weapons and at close proximity. Hannah, Daughter of Mattathias, son of Yochanan, exposed herself to her wedding guests in order to call attention to the outlanders' wicked custom. Those homespun Jews were willing to act.

Additionally, we celebrate that the Maccabees refused to yield their Judaism to the wiles of the ruling crowd. No matter how hard the invading alien powers pressed them, including the alien invalidation of basics like Sabbath and like *brit milah*, circumcision, that small band of scholar-warriors held fast to the essence of Judaism. Eventually, they even defeated a mighty military power. Those homespun Jews were willing to act.

Chanukah is a time of miracles. Chanukah is a time of faith. In partnership with The Boss, let's move forward.

Gratitude

So many hands, hearts, and souls are outstretched this time of the year asking, begging, beseeching. It is expected of us that during the High Holy Days, that we will be pleading with The Blessed Name to sign and seal us in the Book of Life and to take away any harsh decrees otherwise meant for us. Yet, it is likewise suitable for us to use this period to express thanks.

There are many kinds of prayers, all of which we use regularly, including but not limited to the words we speak from our lips and from our hearts on Yom Kippur. On this holy day, we give over: supplication, praise, contrition, and appreciation.

In spite of that veracity, too often, we forget to employ the last of these types of prayer. We err in this way, even during this auspicious season, when, in addition to repentance and charity, our spiritual communications might mean the difference, literally, between life and death.

It behooves us to immerse ourselves in gratitude. From the prayers of thanks that we give over, daily, in the ritualized form of the *"Birchot HaShachar,"* "The Morning Blessings," to the less regular and the more fleeting realizations of goodness, which we might intermittently have of the deeds of loving kindness that surrounds us, we are accustomed to expressing some measure of indebtedness. The former fills our minutes as regularly as does the *"Shema,"* the Jewish confession of faith, while the latter colors our breath when we, for instance, view: a sunset, a beautiful person, or a flowering shrub. Both are relatively ordinary parts of our lives.

Even so, there exists more than those aforementioned kinds of established moments for recognizing The Boss's sympathy toward us. The Lord of the World's benevolence extends much farther than can any sensory delight that we enjoy.

Whereas it is fitting to thank Him for our food, for the music we perform or witness, for the softness of our children and grandchildren's kisses, for the perfume of our gardens, and for each and every sunset and sunrise to which we are privy, it is likewise necessary and appropriate to thank Him for every bit of willingness we find to face the difficulties that daunt us, every bit of encouragement of which we are aware when we brush ourselves off following psychological faltering, and every bit of renewal that we experience when an old year sloughs off and a new one takes its place.

The universe could have been fashioned in such a manner as to leave us without hope of change, of improvement, or of personal growth. The tallies of our deeds, words, and thoughts could have been destined to be lifelong, rather than yearlong. We could have, as well, been created in such a way as to be stuck in whatever mistakes in which we had elected to engage.

However, with much love, G-d built a reality in which it is, and will continue to be, possible to change, to get closer to Him and to live more accordingly to His will. That quality of the nature of being is worth a lifetime of gratefulness.

Granted, Yom Kippur is a physically strenuous day. Folk get hungry. Folk get thirsty. Folk get tired from so much standing, bowing, and sitting ever so still.

Also true is that Yom Kippur is a frightening time. We are faced with our mortality, and, to a lesser extent, although very significant extent, with the frailty of the certainty of our health, of our livelihoods, and of other facets of our well-being.

Nonetheless, Yom Kippur remains, at least equally, an exhilarating day. On this occasion, devoid of as many corporeal distractions as possible, we have a rare potential to lift our souls as high as possible and as close as possible to the Almighty's throne.

In that place of The Name, our large grievances are able to shrink to small ones, and our small ones are able to become dust which, in turn, can easily be blown away. There, in the center of the universe, we can bask in the perfection that is G-d's, alone. We can warm our innermost essences as we prepare for another year of battling the evil inclination. Infused with Our Father's tenderness, accordingly, we can evolve.

Yom Kippur might be The Day of Atonement, but this twenty-five hour period is, as well, the Sabbath of Shabbaths, the apex of an entire calendar's worth of months, a singularity during which we are able to reach, with all of our hearts, with all of our souls, and with all of our might, to say "thank-you" to our Creator. Twelve more months will come and go before we achieve this apex again.

Acknowledgments

Without The Name, we wouldn't breathe, we wouldn't walk, and we wouldn't exist. I hope, daily, to remember my gratitude to our Creator.

End Notes

1. Naftali Kalfa. Personal Interview. July 2012.

2. Ibid.

3. Ibid.

4. Ibid.

5. Ibid.

6. Ibid.

7. Ibid.

8. Ibid.

9. Ibid.

10. Ibid.

11. Moshe Bogomilsky, "Questions and Answers on Chapter One of *Pirkei Avot*." Chabad.org. n.d. Retrieved Nov. 24, 2019. https://www.chabad.org/library/article_cdo/aid/2835298/jewish/Chapter-One.htm.

12. Joel Lurie Grishaver, *Teaching Jewishly*. Los Angeles, CA: Torah Aura Productions, 2001.

13. Rabbi Arthur Segal. "Jewish Spiritual Renewal: Derek Eretz Zuta + Rabbah." *Rabbi Arthur Segal*. Jul. 27, 2011. Retrieved Nov. 24, 2019. http://rabbiarthursegal.blogspot.com/2011/07/rabbi-arthur-segal-derek-eretz-zuta.html.

14. Rabbi Pinchas Avruch. "Investment Strategy: *Parshas Shoftim*." "Kol HaKollel." *Torah.org*. Sep. 9, 2005. Retrieved Nov. 24, 2019. https://torah.org/torah-portion/kolhakollel-5765-shoftim/.

15. Rabbi David Rosenfeld. "Chapter 2: Mishna 14(b): Peer Pressure." "Pirkei Avos." *Torah.org*. Aug. 3, 2017. Retrieved Nov. 24, 2019. https://torah.org/learning/pirkei-avos-chapter2-14b/.

16. Emuna Braverman."Friendship & Empathy." *Aish.com*. Oct. 23, 2011. Retrieved Nov. 24, 2019. https://www.aish.com/f/mom/Friendship__Empathy.html.

17. Rabbi Lazer Brody, "Counting the Omer." *Lazer Beams: Emuna, Geula and Body-Soul Health with Rabbi Lazer Brody*. Apr. 15, 2012. Retrieved Feb. 6, 2019. https://lazerbrody.typepad.com/lazer_beams/2012/04/counting_the_om.html

18. Rav. Saul. Wagschal, *Guide to Derech Eretz*. Spring Valley, New York: Feldheim Publishers, 1993.

19. Moses Schonfeld, ed., *Pirkei Avos*. New York: Behrman House Inc., 1945.

20. Mendel Weinbach, ed., *Give Us Life: Moesholim and Masterwords of the Chofetz Chaim*. Jerusalem: Shma Yisroel Program and Publications, 1973.

21. Ibid.

22. Rav Chaim of Volozhin, *Nefesh Hachaim: Rav Chaim of Volozhin's Classic Exploration of the Fundamentals of Jewish Belief*. Trans. Rabbi Avraham Yaakov Finkel. New York: Judaica Press, 2009. Qtd. in "Chapter 3: Mishna 3: Part 1." Torah.org. 2019. Retrieved Feb. 10, 2019. https://torah.org/learning/maharalp3m3part1

23. Rabbi Simon Jacobson,"To Love and Be Loved: Relationships Secrets Unplugged." YouTube. Dec. 12, 2017. Retrieved Feb. 6, 2019. https://www.youtube.com/watch?v=EKH9C0CJNKw

24. Rabbi Julian Sinclair, "Sinat Chinam." *The Jewish Chronicle*. Mar. 6, 2009.

25. Paul E. Mullen and Jillian Fleming, "Long-Term Effects of Child Sexual Abuse." *Australian Government National Child Protection Clearinghouse*. Apr. 1998. Retrieved Feb, 10, 2019. https://aifs.gov.au/cfca/publications/long-term-effects-childsexual-abuse-1998

26. Jeanne and Robert Segal, "Recognizing and Preventing Child Abuse." Helpguide.org. Rev. Nov. 2018. Retrieved Feb. 10, 2019. https://www.helpguide.org/articles/abuse/child-abuse-and-neglect.htm.

27. Ibid.

28. Ibid.

29. David L. Calof, "Adult Survivors of Incest and Child Abuse, Part One: The Family Inside the Adult Child." *Family Therapy Today*. Van Nuys, CA. P. M. Inc., 1988. Qtd. in Pat McClendon. "Systems Theory and Incest/Sexual Abuse of Children: Focus on Families and Communities." *Pat McClendon's Clinical Social Work*. Fall 1991. Retrieved Feb. 10, 2019. http://www.clinicalsocialworker.com/systems.html.

Bibliography

Avruch, Rabbi Pinchas. "Investment Strategy - Parshas Shoftim," Torah.org, Series Kol HaKollel, September 9, 2005. Retrieved Nov. 24, 2019. https://torah.org/torah-portion/kolhakollel-5765-shoftim/.

Bogomilsky, Moshe. "Questions and Answers on Chapter One of Pirkei Avot," Chabad.org, Retrieved Nov. 24, 2019. https://www.chabad.org/library/article_cdo/aid/2835298/jewish/Chapter-One.htm

Braverman, Emuna."Friendship & Empathy," Aish.com, Oct. 23, 2011. Retrieved Nov. 24, 2019. https://www.aish.com/f/mom/Friendship__Empathy.html

Brody, Rabbi Lazer. "Counting the Omer," Lazer Beams: Emuna, Geula and Body-Soul Health with Rabbi Lazer Brody. Apr. 15, 2012. https://lazerbrody.typepad.com/lazer_beams/2012/04/counting_the_om.html Retrieved Feb. 6, 2019 (link no longer active and article appears to be archived).

Calof, David L. "Adult Survivors of Incest and Child Abuse, Part One: The Family Inside the Adult Child," *Family Therapy Today*, P. M. Inc., 1988, Van Nuys, CA. Qtd. in "Systems Theory and Incest/Sexual Abuse of Children: Focus on Families and Communities," *Pat McClendon's Clinical Social Work*, by Dr. Patricia D. McClendon, Fall 1991. Retrieved Feb. 10, 2019. http://www.clinicalsocialwork.com/systems.html

Chaim of Volozhin. "Rav. Nefesh Hachaim: Rav Chaim of Volozhin's Classic Exploration of the Fundamentals of Jewish Belief," Trans. Rabbi Avraham Yaakov Finkel. New York: Judaica Press, 2009. Qtd. in "Chapter 3: Mishna 3: Part 1," by Rabbi Shaya Karlinski. Torah.org, Series Maharal, 2019. Retrieved Feb. 10, 2019. https://torah.org/learning/maharal-p3m3part1

Greenberg, KJ Hannah. "A Difficult Confluence of Events." Middle Eastern Musings, *The Jerusalem Post* (Mar. 26, 2012).

———. "*Shidduchim*: A Limited Time Offer." Life with Teens and Twenties, *Natural Jewish Parenting* (Jun. 11, 2012).

———. "A Little Perspective." She Said: She Said, *The Jerusalem Post* (Jul. 14, 2009).

———. "About *Pesach* and Giving Thanks." Life with Teens and Twenties, *Natural Jewish Parenting* (Apr. 18, 2012).

———. "After the Confetti." *Natural Jewish Parenting* (Nov. 11, 2012).

———. "And Then Came Kislev." Middle Eastern Musings, *The Jerusalem Post* (Dec. 5, 2012).

———. "*Ani L'Dodi v'Dodi Li*." Middle Eastern Musings, *The Jerusalem Post* (Sep. 10, 2012).

———. "As Simple as Holding Open a Door." She Said: She Said, *The Jerusalem Post* (Oct. 22, 2009).

———. "Becoming a *Bat Shirut* [sic]." She Said: She Said, *The Jerusalem Post* (Mar 2, 2009).

———. "Who's a Jew, Part VI: Blaring among the Mustards." Middle Eastern Musings, *The Jerusalem Post* (Jan. 17, 2011).

———. "Sabbath Bride." *Natural Jewish Parenting* (Oct. 24, 2012).

———. "*Kallah v'Chatan.*" Middle Eastern Musings, *The Jerusalem Post* (Aug. 26, 2012).

———. "*B'yadei Heaven.*" She Said: She Said, *The Jerusalem Post* (Jul. 28, 2009).

———. "Caterpillars to Butterflies." *Natural Jewish Parenting* (Sep. 4, 2012).

———. "Concentric *Yiddishe* Circles." "Middle Eastern Musings." *The Jerusalem Post* (Nov. 23, 2011).

———. "Controlling Attribution of Meaning and Other Lizardly Behaviors." Old/New World Discourse, *The Jerusalem Post* (Dec. 3, 2006).

———. "*Hashgacha Pratis.*" Middle Eastern Musings, *The Jerusalem Post* (Jul. 4, 2012).

———. "Educational Treasure." Old/New World Discourse, *The Jerusalem Post (*Jan. 17, 2007).

———. "Effort, not Outcome." Middle Eastern Musings, *The Jerusalem Post* (Jun. 19, 2011).

———. "Embracing Guilt-free Alternatives to Mainstream Torah Schooling." Life with Teens and Twenties, *Natural Jewish Parenting* (Nov. 20, 2011).

———. "'Ephraim' and 'Manasseh.'" Middle Eastern Musings, *The Jerusalem Post* (Dec. 26, 2011).

———. "First be a *Mensch*: *Derech Eretz Kadma l'Torah.*" Middle Eastern Musings, *The Jerusalem Post* (Mar. 1, 2012).

———. "Friends." Middle Eastern Musings, *The Jerusalem Post* (May 9, 2012).

———. "From under a Rock." Middle Eastern Musings, *The Jerusalem Post* (Jan. 9, 2012).

———. "*Kiruv* and Gefilte Fish." Middle Eastern Musings, *The Jerusalem Post* (Jun. 11, 2012).

———. "Gratitude." Middle Eastern Musings, *The Jerusalem Post* (Oct. 5, 2011).

———. "Growing Up." Middle Eastern Musings, *The Jerusalem Post* (May 13, 2012).

———. "Her Striped Bathrobe." *Natural Jewish Parenting* (Sep. 28, 2012).

———. "Holiday Joy." Middle Eastern Musings, *The Jerusalem Post* (Sep. 30, 2012).

———. "Idiot Drivers and Car Horns." She Said: She Said, *The Jerusalem Post* (Feb. 22, 2009).

———. "I'm Okay, You're Okay, but Bring OU." Middle Eastern Musings, *The Jerusalem Post* (Oct. 30, 2011).

———. "Anniversary Special." Old/New World Discourse, *The Jerusalem Post* (Aug. 6, 2008).

———. "Smile and Nod." She Said: She Said, *The Jerusalem Post* (Sept. 13, 2009).

———. "Keeping House during a Sudden Illness." She Said: She Said, *The Jerusalem Post* (Mar. 24, 2009).

———. "Grateful to be a Jew, Part Three: It Would Have Been Enough: Gratitude for My Learning Partners." Middle Eastern Musings, *The Jerusalem Post* (May 13, 2011).

———. "Looking Forward: Looking Backward." Life with Teens and Twenties, *Natural Jewish Parenting* (Dec. 9, 2012).

———. "Loud and Soft: Stepping Toward Yom Kippur." Middle Eastern Musings, *The Jerusalem Post* (Sep. 23, 2012).

———. "*Shana Tova*: Love, not Fear." Middle Eastern Musings, *The Jerusalem Post* (Sep. 16, 2012).

———. "More than a White Gown." Middle Eastern Musings, *The Jerusalem Post* (May 21, 2012).

———. "More Grousing." Middle Eastern Musings, *The Jerusalem Post* (Dec. 9, 2012).

———. "Grateful to be a Jew, Part Six: Neither Location nor *Hashkafa*." Middle Eastern Musings, *The Jerusalem Post* (Jun. 5, 2011).

———. "No More Vegetarian *Shabbatot*." *Natural Jewish Parenting* (Nov. 28, 2012).

———. "Once More Down the Aisle." Middle Eastern Musings, *The Jerusalem Post* (Jun. 24, 2012).

———. "Parenting a Daughter in *Shidduchim*." *Natural Jewish Parenting* (Jul. 22, 2012).

———. "More Passages: Weddings and New Years." *Natural Jewish Parenting* (Sep. 16, 2012).

———. "Pepper and Salt." She Said: She Said, *The Jerusalem Post* (Jun. 23, 2009).

———. "Progress." Life with Teens and Twenties, *Natural Jewish Parenting* (Mar. 25, 2012).

———. "Quietly Now." Middle Eastern Musings, *The Jerusalem Post* (Oct. 10, 2012).

———. "Relative Riches: Familial Transitions." Middle Eastern Musings, *The Jerusalem Post* (Nov. 6, 2011).

———. "Remembering Jeff Zaslow." Middle Eastern Musings, *The Jerusalem Post* (Mar. 18, 2012).

———. "*Shemiras haLoshon*: The Ongoing Importance of Guarding One's Tongue: Part I," "*Shemiras haLoshon*: The Ongoing Importance of Guarding One's Tongue: Part II," and "*Shemiras haLoshon*: The Ongoing Importance of Guarding One's Tongue: Part III." Middle Eastern Musings, *The Jerusalem Post* (Jul. 18, Jul. 23, and Aug. 5, 2012).

———. "Small Packages: The Importance of Seemingly Insignificant Portions." *Natural Jewish Parenting* (Aug. 6, 2012).

———. "Smoldering Dumpsters and Other 'Rhetorical Devices.'" Old/New World Discourse, *The Jerusalem Post* (Nov. 9, 2006).

———. "Who's a Jew, Part Two: So Much Clap-Trap." Middle Eastern Musings, *The Jerusalem Post* (Dec. 22, 2010).

———. "Something Meaningful in the Violence Here." Old/New World Discourse, *The Jerusalem Post* (Oct. 15, 2007).

———. "Starfighters." Life with Teens and Twenties, *Natural Jewish Parenting* (Jan. 2, 2012).

———. "Student Loans and Other *Klita* Fantasies." Old/New World Discourse, *The Jerusalem Post* (Jul. 1, 2008).

———. "Supernal Music." Middle Eastern Musings, *The Jerusalem Post* (Aug. 12, 2012).

———. "Talking Fishes, Fidgety Parrots, and the Rest of the Menagerie." *Natural Jewish Parenting* (Jan. 6, 2013).

———. "The Death of a Dear Friend." She Said: She Said, *The Jerusalem Post* (Aug. 9, 2009).

———. "The Merits of Counting." Middle Eastern Musings, *The Jerusalem Post* (Apr. 24, 2012).

———. "The New Normal." Middle Eastern Musings, *The Jerusalem Post* (Nov. 15, 2012).

———. "The Other Five." Middle Eastern Musings, *The Jerusalem Post* (Nov. 29, 2011).

———. "To the *Chuppah* without Interference." *Natural Jewish Parenting* (Aug. 21, 2012).

———. "Torah Teachers and Other Treasures." Middle Eastern Musings, *The Jerusalem Post* (Aug. 10, 2011).

———. "Transitioning." Middle Eastern Musings, *The Jerusalem Post* (Oct. 19, 2012).

———. "*Achdut*." Middle Eastern Musings, *The Jerusalem Post* (Dec. 5, 2011).

———. "Wardrobe Unsavvy." She Said: She Said, *The Jerusalem Post* (Jan. 29, 2009).

———. "Wedding Countdown: Staying in the Joy." Middle Eastern Musings, *The Jerusalem Post* (Oct. 24, 2012).

Grishaver, Joel Lurie. Teaching Jewishly. Los Angeles, CA: Torah Aura Productions, 2001.

Jacobson, Rabbi Simon. "To Love and Be Loved: Relationships Secrets Unplugged," YouTube. Dec. 12, 2017. Retrieved Feb. 6, 2019. https://www.youtube.com/watch?v=EKH9C0CJNKw

Mullen, Paul E. and Jillian Fleming. "Long-Term Effects of Child Sexual Abuse," Australian Government National Child Protection Clearinghouse, NCPC Issues No. 9. Apr. 1998. Retrieved Feb. 10, 2019. https://aifs.gov.au/cfca/publications/long-term-effects-child-sexual-abuse-1998

Rosenfeld, Rabbi David. "Chapter 2: Mishna 14(b): Peer Pressure." Torah.org, Series Pirkei Avos. Aug. 3, 2017. Retrieved Nov. 24, 2019. https://torah.org/learning/pirkei-avos-chapter2-14b/

Schonfeld, Moses, Ed. Pirkei Avos. New York: Behrman House Inc., 1945.

Segal, Rabbi Arthur. "Jewish Spiritual Renewal: Derek Eretz Zuta + Rabbah." Rabbi Arthur Segal. Jul. 27, 2011. Retrieved Nov. 24, 2019. http://rabbiarthursegal.blogspot.com/2011/07/rabbi-arthur-segal-derek-eretz-zuta.html

Segal, Jeanne, and Robert Segal. "Recognizing and Preventing Child Abuse." Helpguide.org. Rev. Nov. 2018. Retrieved Feb. 10, 2019. https://www.helpguide.org/articles/abuse/child-abuse-and-neglect.htm

Sinclair, Rabbi Julian. "Sinat Chinam." The Jewish Chronicle. Mar. 6, 2009. Retrieved Feb. 6, 2019. https://www.thejc.com/judaism/jewish-words/sinat-chinam-1.8105

Wagschal, Rav. Saul. Guide to Derech Eretz. Spring Valley, New York: Feldheim Publishers, 1993.

Weinbach, Mendel, Ed. Give Us Life: Moesholim and Masterwords of the Chofetz Chaim. Jerusalem: Shma Yisroel Program and Publications, 1973.

About the Authors

National Endowment for the Humanities awardee, wife, and mother, **K.J. Hannah Greenberg** is an author and teacher. Some of the venues for her work have included: *Natural Jewish Parenting, Horizons, The New Vilna Review*, and *The Jerusalem Post*. Her books include *Whistling for Salvation* (Seashell Books, 2019), *On Golden Limestone* (Seashell Books, 2018), *Tosh: Select Trash and Bosh of Creative Writing* (Crooked Cat Books, 2017), *Word Citizen: Uncommon Thoughts on Writing, Motherhood & Life in Jerusalem* (Tailwinds Press, 2015), and *Jerusalem Sunrise* (Imago Press, 2015).

Rivka Gross *nee* Greenberg is a fairly normal twenty-something, all things considered. She writes across the spectrum, penning children's stories about shoe-eating playground monsters and blogging about growing up in a frenetic home. Although she is a high school English teacher, she believes her future ought to include the crocheting of feral animals. Some of the venues for her work include *The Jerusalem Post* and *Chabad.org*.

For memorable fiction, non-fiction, poetry, and prose,
please visit us on the web
www.propertiuspress.com

CPSIA information can be obtained
at www.ICGtesting.com
Printed in the USA
LVHW031927190221
679369LV00004B/251